The T

RORKE'S DRIFT

James W Bancroft

JONATHAN BALL PUBLISHERS
Johannesburg

RORKE'S DRIFT

James W Bancroft

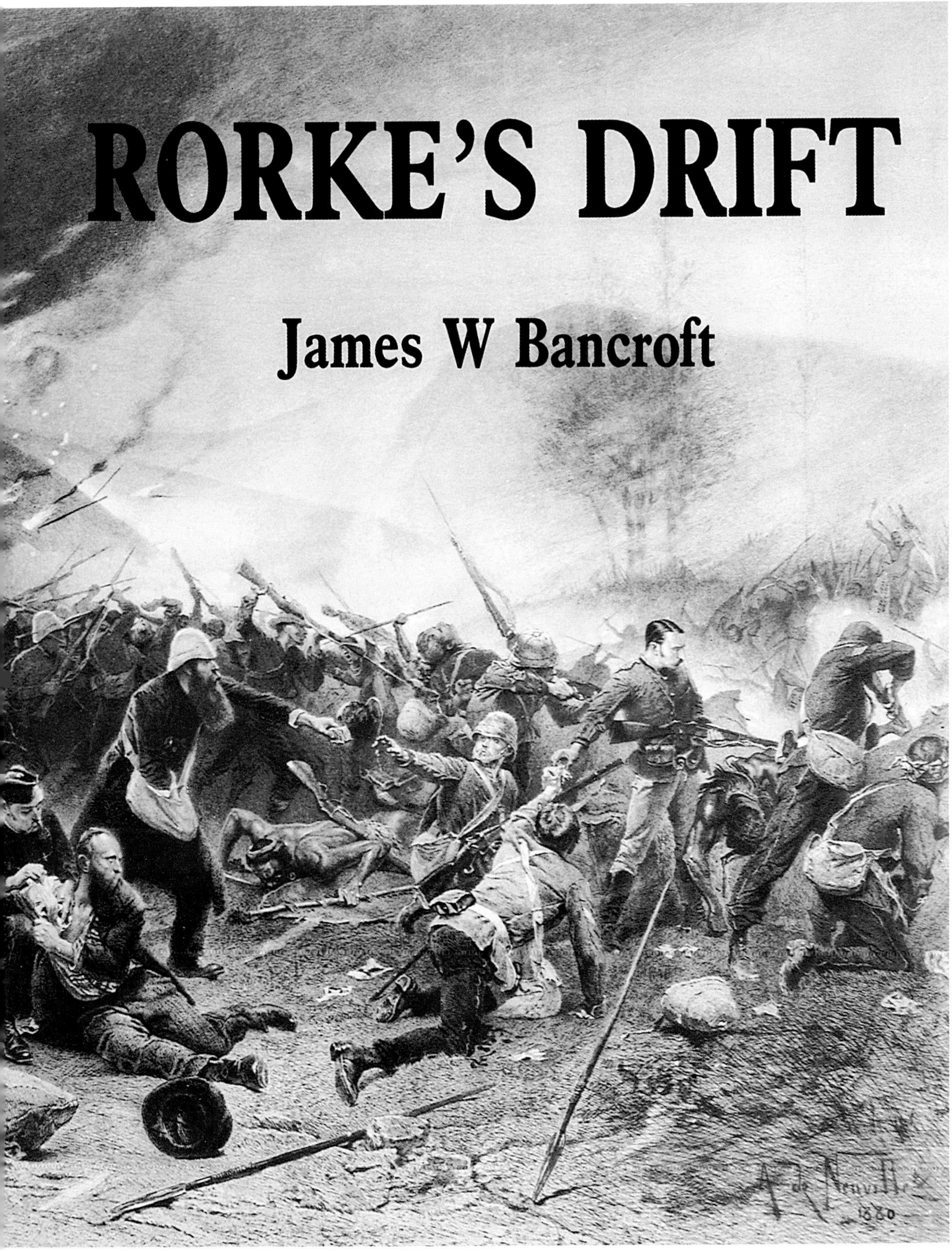

First published in the United Kingdom in hard cover in 1988 by
Spellmount Limited
The Old Rectory
Staplehurst
Kent TN12 0AZ

Published in hard cover in 1997 by
JONATHAN BALL PUBLISHERS (PTY) LTD
P O Box 33977
Jeppestown 2043
South Africa

This edition published in soft cover in 2004

ISBN 1 86842 184 8

Printed and bound in Singapore

The Terrible Night at
RORKE'S DRIFT
The Zulu War, 1879

To
Remind us
Always, that
Courage and
Endurance
Yield success

CHAPTER ONE:
Zulu Defiance

'It is the habit of every aggressor nation to claim that it is acting on the defensive.'
Jawaharlal Nehru

For most of the nineteenth century South Africa was disturbed by continuous friction between its mixed population. After British troops had twice seized the Cape from the Dutch at the turn of the century, settlers began to arrive in 1820, and as they expanded the frontier, there were many disputes over land boundaries between Cape Colonists and African Bantu tribes, which kept the British army on constant alert. These disagreements on occasions led to confrontations that became known as the Kaffir, or Frontier, Wars.

Soon after the British Government had abolished slavery in 1833, Boer farmers who were of Dutch origin, began to push northwards into the interior, to search for land where they could settle independently from British administration at the Cape. These 'Treks' met with resistance from the natives, especially the Zulu, who, because of a series of bloody battles and subsequent reprisals, became their bitter

In this scene of life in a military kraal, Mpande has called forward his finest warriors to perform a ceremonial dance during his review of the troops. They will then take part in a display of combat skills set by the king.

enemies. The Boers continued to push over the Drakensberg mountains, and the British moved across the Great Kei river, which formed the north-east border of Cape Colony, until by the middle of the century the Zulus found their kingdom bordered on the west by The Orange Free State and The Transvaal Republic, both of which had been founded by the Boers, and in the south by the British province of Natal.

Early in the century the Zulus had been disciplined by a great military-minded chief named Shaka. Shaka had been born the illegitimate son of Sezangakhona, chief of the Zulus, and a woman called Nandi from a neighbouring tribe. At that time the Zulus were only one of a number of small Nguni tribes, which also included the Swazi, the Xhosa and the Mthethwa. They lived in the area between the Drakensberg mountains and the south-east coast. Because of the circumstances of his birth, Shaka and his mother led difficult lives as outcasts, and this had a lasting effect on him.

At an early age he began to show great courage and skill with weapons which at that time consisted of a throwing spear and a long, knobble-ended mace, called a *knobkerrie* used for clubbing an opponent. Tales abounded concerning Shaka's prowess. As a herdboy he fought and killed a fierce leopard that had come to attack his cattle. There was also the saga of a mad giant who lived on a hilltop in Shaka's district and for years this warrior would come down to terrorise and plunder the local natives. But one day he chose to approach the herd of cattle

Boer farmers struggle to negotiate a dangerous ridge on the Drakensberg mountains during their legendary 'Great Trek' across the interior veld to establish independence from British domination at the Cape.

that was in Shaka's care. The madman was confronted by the 6 feet 3 inch muscular young man who had, by now, become a proficient fighter. After a duel that was still talked about among the Zulus a hundred years later, Shaka triumphed. He became a fearless warrior, and his skill in battle soon attracted the attention of Dingiswayo, a Mthethwa chieftain with great military talent. Dingiswayo initiated the promising young man into one of his regiments, and in 1818 he was instrumental in making him ruler of the Zulus.

Shaka learned the advantages of an organised regimental system from Dingiswayo. As soon as young Zulus reached their teens they were put into age-regiments, led by chiefs, or *inDuna*s, chosen by Shaka. Regiments of old warriors and regiments made up of young warriors were combined to form a Corps, thus enabling the new recruits to learn from the experiences of the older men, and eventually to take their place. Each regiment had its own distinctive style of war regalia, and the warriors lived in military stockades, segregated from the domestic settlements. Shaka assured aggression in his warriors by depriving them of female companionship for long periods. And the fact that warriors who had been defeated in battle were put to death on their return, also considerably enhanced their determination for victory. Killing became a custom of the Zulu nation, and 'To Conquer Or To Die' became their motto. The warriors were not allowed to marry without the permission of the king, and this was not given until they had fought in battle and 'washed their spears' in human blood. The regiments who had proved themselves and had been allowed to marry, carried light-coloured shields, and wore a head-ring, or *isiCoco*, woven into the hair at the crown of their heads.

Shaka was a tall, powerful figure, who ruled his people with an iron fist. His dreaded army slaughtered thousands of Bantu tribesmen during the Zulu rise to greatness. But he sealed his fate when he began to exterminate his own subjects.

Shaka also made revolutionary improvements to their weaponry. He was an expert with the throwing spear, but he was not impressed by its effectiveness. He had noticed in battles that no real harm was done to an enemy until his warriors had closed on them. And the spears could be picked up by an opponent and thrown back. So he rearmed his regiments with short, broad-bladed stabbing spears called *assegai*s. These required very close combat, so swiftness of foot was important. Shaka believed that bare feet could move more surely across the hard rocky ground, so he ordered his warriors to discard their sandals. Some men disapproved, because the terrain was also very thorny. Shaka solved this problem by ordering them to prepare beds of thorns on the ground, and to harden their feet by repeatedly marching over them.

Tribal warfare had always, until then, been fought without any basic organisation. But Shaka introduced a tactical fighting formation based on an old hunting technique. His army, known as an *impi*, was divided into four groups. The bulk of the warriors formed a central group – the chest – that first engaged the enemy. Then two groups – the horns – swiftly moved round on each side to attack the flanks and rear, and encircle them. A reserve force – the loins – was kept at the rear, ready to be used if

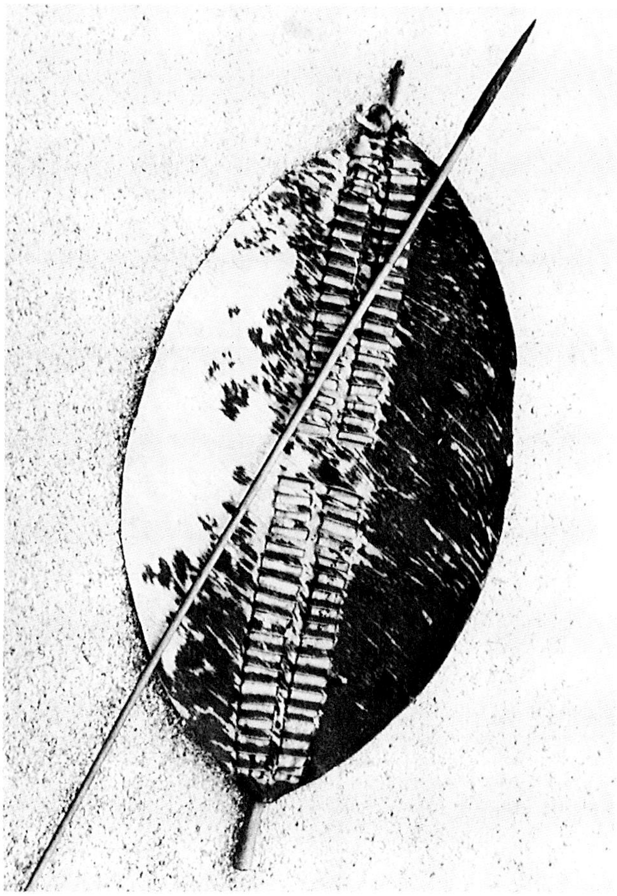

Left: *A throwing spear and the small cowhide shield adopted in the mid-1850's. The shield was designed to allow the warrior more mobility, while still providing protection in battle.*

Right: *The exotic bird plumes and feather, with otterskin headband and loincloth incorporated in this warrior's war regalia makes him distinguishable to his regiment. His dress blends with his surroundings, although he may have discarded some of the regalia when he went into combat.*

Below: *The assegai was grasped by the hand grip and thrust forward in an underarm movement. When carrying the knobkerrie mace in addition to the simple but effective weapons shown on this page, the Zulu warrior was a formidable foe in tribal warfare.*

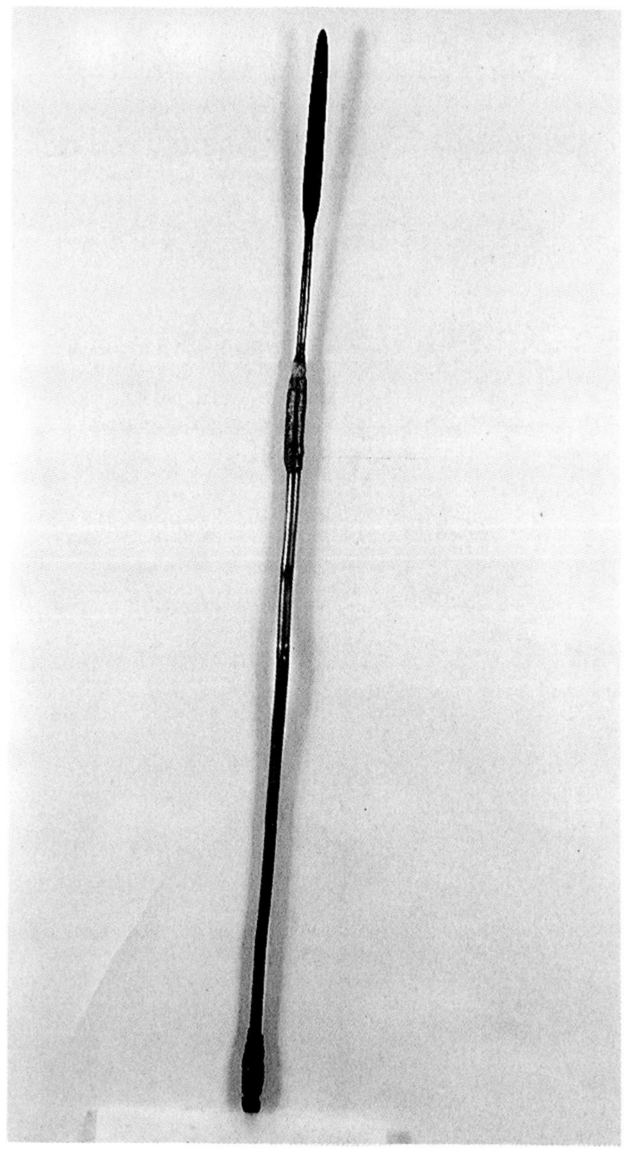

needed. Shaka's tough and bold warriors were well drilled with their weapons, and disciplined in battle. They slept naked on military expeditions, whatever the weather. The King revenged himself on those who had treated his mother badly, and one by one the Bantu tribes were crushed. The Zulu took possession of all conquered land. Any courageous warriors lucky enough to survive a battle were incorporated into the Zulu regiments. Within four years the land of the *amaZulu* – 'The children of the heavens' – covered over 20,000 square miles!

Shaka led the Zulus to greatness, but eventually his rule became one of terror. With no tribes remaining prepared to urge war against his superior forces, he had no means by which to relieve his aggressive feelings. He began to commit needless atrocities on his own people. He executed four hundred women on suspicion of witchcraft, and any shield-bearer who allowed a ray of sunlight to fall on him while he was shading him from its glare, was killed. And yet there was no shortage of men willing to take over the honour of shading the royal head. There was security in having a feared king, and the Zulu people were prepared to put up with their precari-

King Mpande was a weak ruler by Zulu standards, but he upheld some of the harsh traditions passed down the generations. He is seen here sitting in state outside his harem. He is protected from the sun by his shield bearer, whose own future was not bright if he allowed a ray of sunlight to shine on the royal head.

ous existence, so long as they knew that Shaka commanded the reputation of a powerful leader. But after his mother Nandi died in 1827, he brooded, and even began to lose the respect that he had built up for himself. He executed anyone who did not show continual grief at her death, and subjected his people to long periods of fasting. Sex was banned for a year, and the meaningless slaughters went on. He put to death anyone who sneezed while he was eating, and cut open a hundred pregnant women during a fad he had for embryology. At last the Zulu could stand it no longer, and in 1828 some of his own family, including his successor Dingane, conspired to stab him to death.

It was during Dingane's reign that the Zulus had started to resist the expansionist Boer republics. But he and his successor Mpande, who came to the throne in 1840, relaxed the strict military traditions. Mpande had not been king long before his family were squabbling about who would succeed him. Eventually Cetshwayo and Mbalini were the two men who emerged as the main rivals for the throne. The dispute was decided in 1856, when Cetshwayo's 20,000 Usuthu warriors pursued Mbalini's isiGqoza faction of about 30,000 men, women and children, including five more of Mpande's sons, until they trapped them at the river near the Ndondakusuka kraal. What followed was one of the most shocking massacres in Zulu history.

Mpande died in 1872, and Cetshwayo was crowned king of Zululand in the following year. He was a cunningly prudent leader. He hated the way his father had allowed the Zulu to lose their military reputation, and loved to hear stories of the great Shaka period. Under his leadership the Zulu army again became great. He added new regiments, and by 1878 these numbered thirty-three.

Although the main structure of Zulu life was built on military lines, Cetshwayo did not keep a standing army as Shaka had done. Except for his personal bodyguard, most of his warriors enjoyed a comfortable life farming the fertile coastal land, that with a fine sub-tropical climate endorsed with a regular rainfall, was perfect for agriculture and grazing sheep and cattle. They lived in circular homesteads called kraals, with dome-shaped thatched huts, each kraal being governed domestically by an inDuna. The king had become mainly a figurehead to whom the inDunas usually stayed loyal.

The women spent their day repairing basketwork for the huts, or preparing food. Some also boiled millet to make beer, or picked leaves to make pipe tobacco or snuff. When the men were not working the land they were kept in shape by regular military exercises, which now included learning to use the firearms that Cetshwayo acquired from white traders. But a Zulu warrior still prided himself on his ability to fight in close-combat, and was always restless to gain military honour. They saw themselves as invincible, and among the local native tribes they were. Cetshwayo had as many as 40,000 of these efficient warriors at his disposal, and this threat naturally caused great unease among his European neighbours.

Cetshwayo ka Mpande patterned his mode of rule on that of Shaka, being more intelligent and at times equally ruthless. He strengthened his army to retain independence for the Zulu, but when his kingdom became the main obstacle to confederation, the British invaded.

While it was a great honour for a young Zulu to reach the age when he could join a regiment, a Briton took the Queen's shilling as a last resort, usually when he could not find work. Redcoats were mostly looked upon as social outcasts, and usually came from the lower classes. Many were unskilled factory workers, farm labourers, or petty criminals, who joined at the police courts to save themselves from being thrown into jail.

In 1879 the British army included over a hundred numbered line-regiments, made up of eight companies lettered from A to H. The first twenty-five had two battalions. In 1871-72 the Secretary of State for War, Lord Cardwell, introduced a number of reforms. The branding of deserters was stopped in 1871, and commission by purchase was abolished in 1872. He introduced the retirement of officers, and the short service system, whereby a soldier could serve for three years with the colours, and then transfer to the army reserve for another five, giving married men the opportunity to spend more time close to home. But the soldier still had to serve for twenty-one years to qualify for a pension. The building of new depots and the introduction of cookhouses made life healthier for the rank and file. But army life was still tough and disciplined. Scrawny lads from city slums found themselves developing more respect for their personal cleanliness and domestic hygiene. The army made them into men. Each company lived, ate, and slept in the same barrack room, and they became a closely-knit unit. Their day was filled with drill on the parade ground, fatigues, such as scrubbing out the barrack block, and guard duty. A soldier caught napping on duty could still be severely flogged. Wages were a shilling a day, with half deducted for luxuries such as extra rations and laundry. The rest was usually spent on recreation, such as drinking heavily, picking up loose women in the nearest town, and ending the evening brawling with members of a rival regiment. In some cases battalions of the same regiment could not be trusted together.

There were fine traditions and staunch loyalties and, overall, officers had complete faith in the steadfastness of the British soldier. But ideas had changed little since Waterloo, and methods of training and tactics had become outdated. The professional British army owed its existence to the Empire, and it guarded it well. The 'British square' where ranks of soldiers stood shoulder to shoulder and maintained a continuous fire, was effective against a

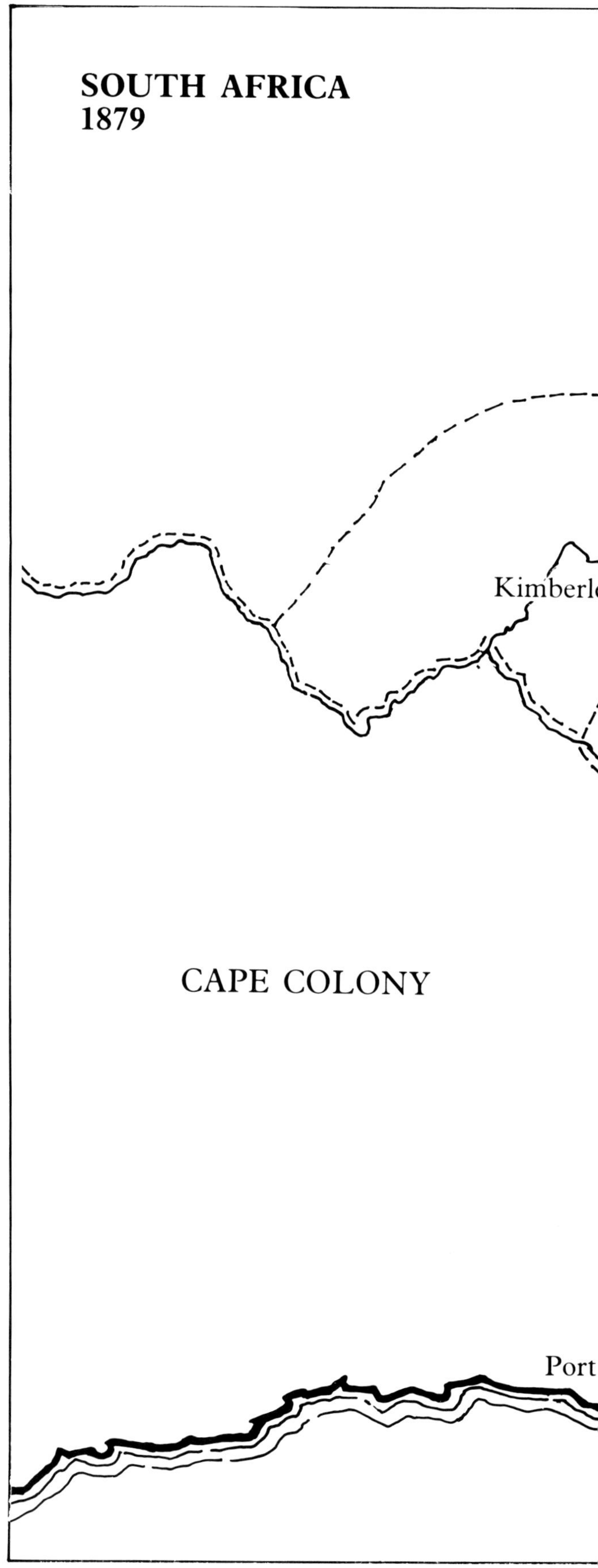

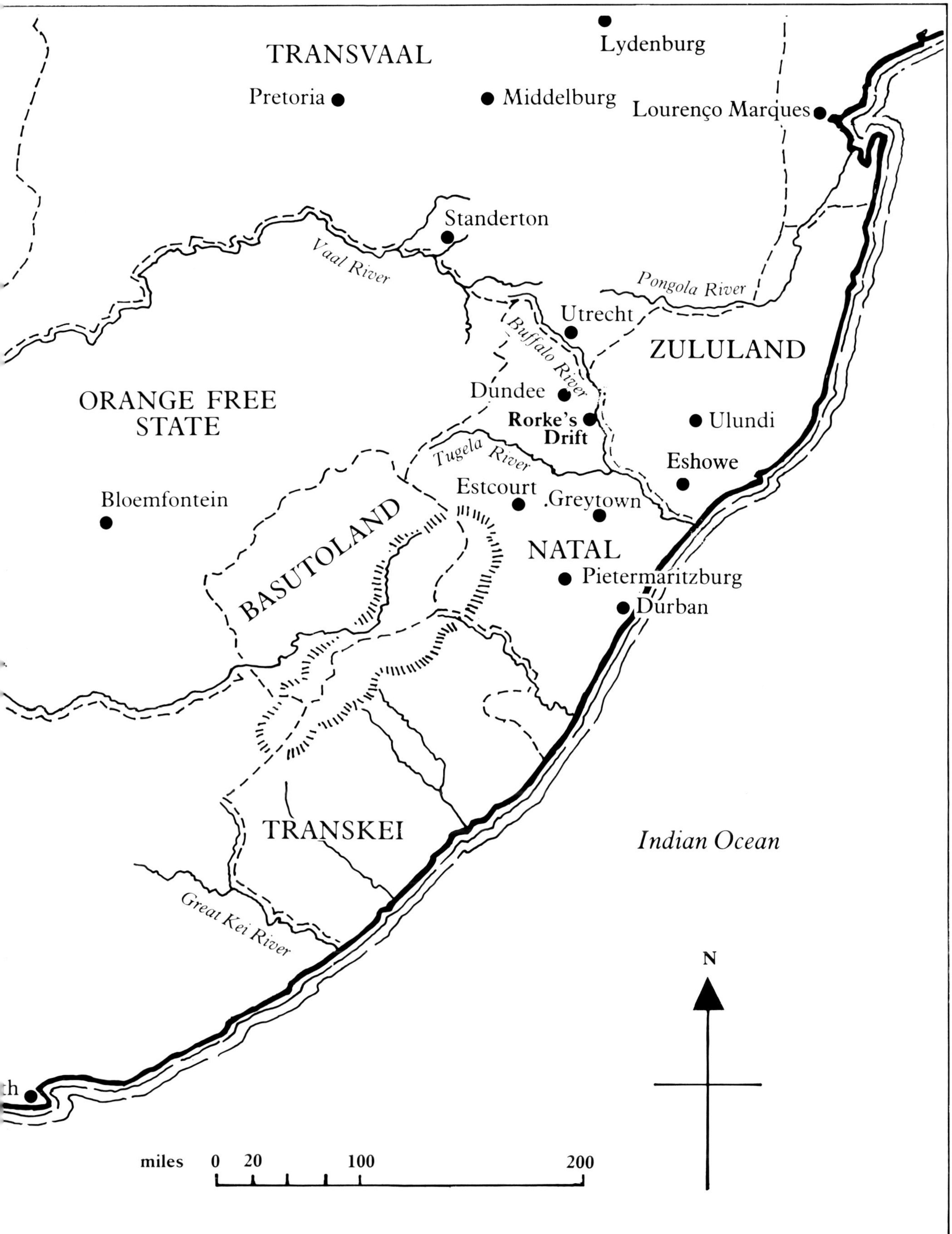
TRANSVAAL
Lydenburg
Pretoria
Middelburg
Lourenço Marques
Standerton
Vaal River
Pongola River
Utrecht
Buffalo River
ZULULAND
ORANGE FREE STATE
Dundee
Rorke's Drift
Ulundi
Tugela River
Eshowe
Bloemfontein
Estcourt
Greytown
BASUTOLAND
NATAL
Pietermaritzburg
Durban
TRANSKEI
Indian Ocean
Great Kei River
N
miles 0 20 100 200

charging enemy armed with the relatively primitive weapons from 60 years before. But modern European armies had begun to introduce tactical stratagems such as using small, detached units, making use of cover. Successive British governments were reluctant to spend money on the army, and even more so in South Africa, once the Suez Canal opened in 1869 and shortened the passage to India.

British administration in South Africa, after years of endless squabbles and requests for the protection of the crown, tried to put in motion an idea that it had been considering for years, a plan to bring all the races together into one confederation under British rule. Most of the European colonists disliked the idea. Cape colonists had no desire to take on their less fortunate squabbling neighbours, and the Boers had no intention of losing the independence for which they had fought and died. To add to this, there were still many territorial disputes that would have to be settled before any form of legislation could be implemented. One such dispute between the Transvaal Boers and Sekukuni, chief of the Bpedi tribe, centred on an area near the Blood river. Sekukuni claimed the land and in 1876 his warriors repulsed a Boer force, and then took refuge in a stronghold in the Transvaal mountains. From there he sent out raiding parties to plunder the area.

In 1877 the reluctant, but bankrupt, Boer state was annexed to Britain, and the Sekukuni problem became the responsibility of the Crown. But he continued to resist all efforts to force him out. Sekukuni was known to be an ally of Cetshwayo, and there were all the signs that other native clans were going to rebel. The British suspected that Cetshwayo was encouraging their defiance. Zulu power would have to be dealt with. The desire for a Confederation of states, including Zululand, and the wishes of the restless Zulu warriors to wash their spears meant that some kind of conflict was inevitable.

In February 1878, the 2nd Bn, 24th (2nd Warwickshire) Regt, received orders to move from Chatham to Plymouth, where they were to board the troop-ship *Himalaya*, and sail to South Africa. There they would join their 1st Bn for active service in the 9th Frontier War at the Cape.

The battalion was first organised in Sheffield in 1858, and presented with colours the following year. Its first tour of overseas duty was on the sugar island of Mauritius in the Indian Ocean, from 1860 until 1865, and it had then served in Burma until it arrived back in the new depot at Brecon in 1873. Since then it had been at home, but the 1st Bn had been at the Cape since 1874. It had served in Griqualand in 1875, and had been involved in several other disturbances. But many of the soldiers of the 2nd Bn were young men fresh from the farms and factories of Britain.

The month long voyage to the Cape in cramped conditions was wearisome. After drill and kit inspection, the soldiers spent their time playing table games, or just staring out to sea with thoughts of family and girlfriends. In the evening it was impossible to move about freely on the troop-deck, because of the vast number of low-swinging hammocks and sleeping bodies on the floor.

HMS Himalaya served the British army for many years. It was used to sail troops to the Crimea and transported the 2/24th Regiment to South Africa.

After their arrival at the Cape, the troops were transported to King William's Town in the north-eastern Cape, the most advanced post in the area of unrest where the Gaika and Gcaleka tribes were causing problems. The campaign followed the usual pattern of kaffir disturbances: the rebels used the bushy terrain for refuge and extended lines of troops entered the scrub to flush them out. By June, Sindali, chief of the Gaikas had been killed, and the Gcaleka chief, Kreli, had been captured. The rebels lost heart, and the uprising was over. These sweeping skirmishes in the Perie Bush gave the 2nd Bn their first experience of active service.

Lt-Gen Sir Frederic Thesiger, soon to become the 2nd Baron Chelmsford, was Commander-in-Chief of the British forces in South Africa. He now turned his attentions to the 'arrogant' Cetshwayo and the Zulu problem. A coastal mail-steamer took the 24th Regt to Natal and on to Fort Napier, Pietermaritzburg to prepare for war.

A series of incidents then occurred. Cetshwayo had little understanding of the principles of European law and simply thought that if he did not show hostility towards the British they would have no reason to quarrel with him. A number of aggressive outbursts in defence of his opinions provoked the British. Zulus were marauding across the northern border into Swaziland, and there were signs that the *impis* were growing restless. There were reports that they had actually begun to fight amongst themselves. On the 28th July 1878, a dispute within the family of an InDuna called Sihayo kaXonga, chief of the Qungebe tribe, whose kraal was only four miles from the border with Natal, resulted in what was considered to be the unlawful killing of two of his adulterous wives, and violations of British territory by the family factions.

The governor of the Cape, Sir Henry Bartle-Frere prepared an ultimatum, that was deliberately unworkably harsh. On the 11th December Zulu emissaries came to the border to hear the results of a boundary commission which found that the Zulu claim was justified. But the ultimatum was also put to them. It requested the turning over of Sihayo's sons, who were the culprits, and a large fine in livestock. It also contained various extra clauses, including demands that the Zulu army must be disbanded, and the warriors made free to marry. This was to be answered before the first day of 1879.

Cetshwayo and his councillors were divided in their opinions of how to react to the ultimatum. The offenders of the border incursion had fled to the north, and Sihayo refused to betray them. So Cetshwayo began to gather livestock to send on his behalf. However, he knew that to accept the terms would mean the loss of Zulu independence, and the ultimate breakdown of Zulu society.

No reply to the ultimatum was received from the Zulu king after twenty days, so a further ten days' grace was allowed. This expired at midnight on Friday, 10th January, 1879.

The border commission present Sir Henry Bartle-Frere's fateful ultimatum to Cetshwayo's representatives beneath the shadow of a tree on the banks of the Lower Tugela River.

CHAPTER TWO:
The Wild Frontier

'If our time is come, let us die manfully for our brethren's sake, and not have cause of reproach against our glory.'
1. Macc. ix. 10.

British troops gradually made their way towards the border, and Zulu scouts warned Cetshwayo of the build-up of forces along the frontier. The total number of men under Lord Chelmsford's command was 5,400 Imperial soldiers, 1,200 colonial volunteers and 10,000 Natal natives. He also had a thousand transport vehicles at his disposal. To enter Zululand along the narrow tracks with such a convoy of men and wagons would be impossible. So he decided to divide his troops into five sections. His plan of action was almost the same tactic as the chest and horns formation used by the Zulus. Three main columns were to enter Zululand at different points along the border, and advance towards the royal kraal at Ulundi, about seventy-five miles away by the tracks. Two reserve forces would stay on the near side of the river to watch the frontier. This, he believed, would tie-down all the Zulu regi-

A view across the Buffalo River from the area around Rorke's Drift, which would have been the scene of the central column advance into Zululand. Isandhlwana Hill is visible in the distance.

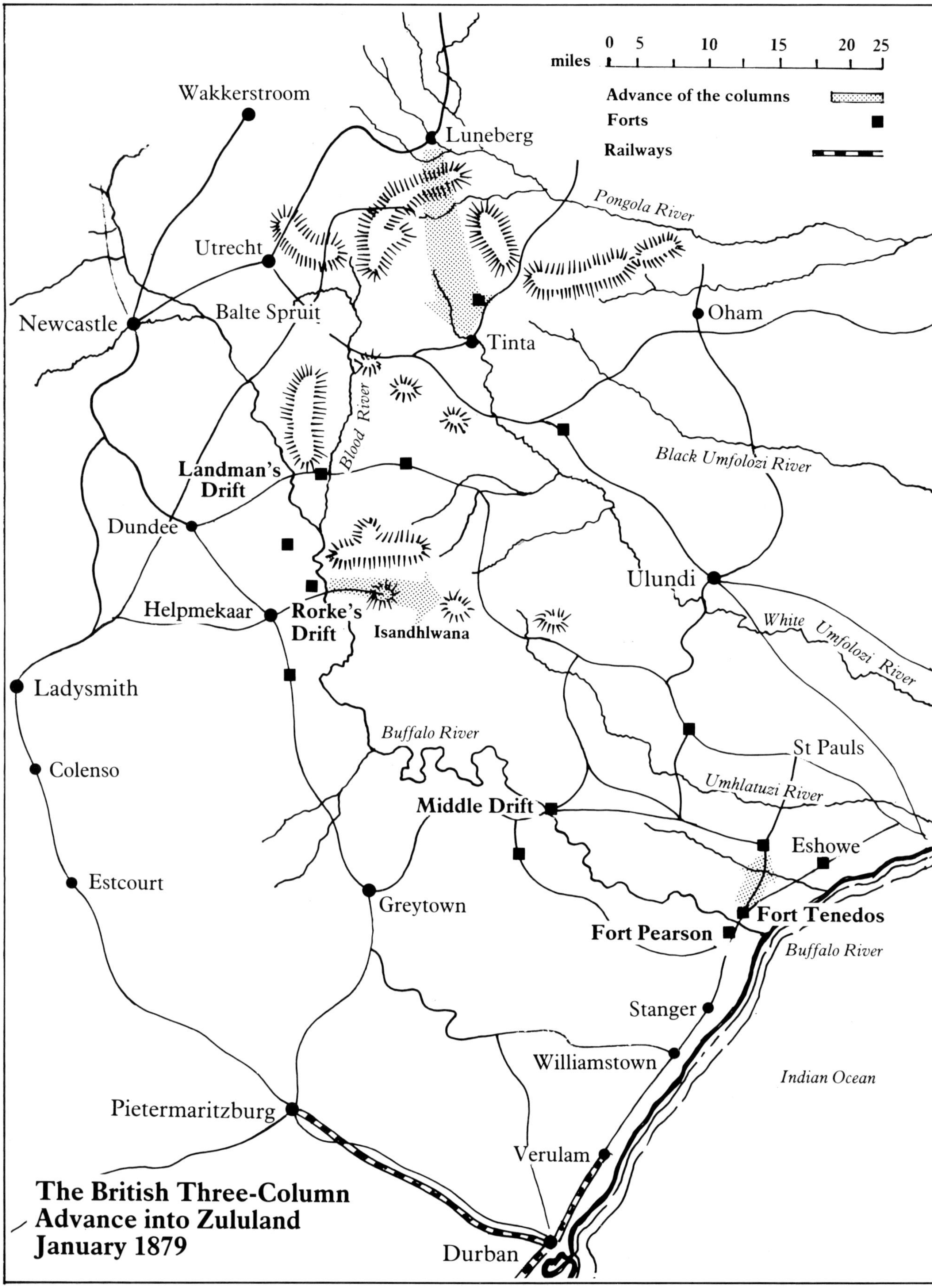
0 5 10 15 20 25
miles
Advance of the columns
Forts
Railways
Wakkerstroom
Luneberg
Pongola River
Utrecht
Newcastle
Balte Spruit
Tinta
Oham
Blood River
Landman's Drift
Black Umfolozi River
Dundee
Ulundi
Helpmekaar
Rorke's Drift
Isandhlwana
White Umfolozi River
Ladysmith
Buffalo River
St Pauls
Colenso
Umhlatuzi River
Middle Drift
Eshowe
Estcourt
Greytown
Fort Tenedos
Fort Pearson
Buffalo River
Stanger
Williamstown
Indian Ocean
Pietermaritzburg
Verulam
Durban
The British Three-Column
Advance into Zululand
January 1879

ments, and thus prevent any counter-strike into British territory.

Col Charles Pearson, 3rd Buffs, was to command a column that was to cross the border near the mouth of the Tugela river, and camp at a Norwegian mission-station near the town of Eshowe, in southern Zululand. He was to wait for a progress report on the other two columns before advancing further. Col Evelyn Wood VC, 90th Light Infantry, would advance his column from Utrecht in the Transvaal, across the Blood river, and move towards Ulundi via Khambula Hill, twenty miles from the border. He was to keep in contact as much as possible with Lord Chelmsford, who had attached himself to the Central, or 3rd Column, commanded by Lt-Col Richard Glyn, CB of the 24th Regt, which was to cross the Buffalo river at a place called Rorke's Drift. Col Anthony Durnford, RE kept a force of mounted volunteers, and colonial natives at the middle-drift of the Tugela, with orders to stay on the south side of the river. Another reserve section under Col Hugh Rowlands VC, 41st Regt, was camped at Luneberg in the Transvaal, to keep an eye on Sekukuni, and any possibility of a Boer extremist uprising while the British troops were preoccupied in Zululand.

It was considered that all three main columns were strong enough to withstand anything that Cetshwayo could send against them. But an army marches on its stomach, and Lord Chelmsford's problems were with the marshalling of transport and supplies, another factor that had dictated his need to split the troops. The transport consisted of Cape wagons that were eighteen feet long and were awkward and heavy when loaded. Even with eighteen oxen to pull just one of them, they could be stopped by the slightest ridge or soggy patch of track. Zululand was a maze of *dongas* (steep-sided water courses), with sudden high ridges and unpredictable marshlands, that could be a muddy quagmire after a morning downpour, becoming hard and dusty under the sweltering mid-afternoon sun. The tracks were rough and bumpy, and the sudden, heavy thunderstorms could swell a river and make the crossing treacherous if not impossible.

With all these points in mind, the British could hardly chase after an army as mobile as the Zulus who were capable of running from the capital to the border in less than two days, and could go for days without food. The only safe way of moving the columns was to establish several base camps during the

Above: *Lt-Col Glyn of the 24th Regiment, who commanded the 3rd column, was known to be a grouchy, quarrelsome man, and may have resented the Commander-in-Chief's presence with the forces under his command.*

Below: *A colonial covered ox-wagon typical of those used by the British invasion force. With an average unladen weight of nearly thirty hundredweight, it took between sixteen and twenty oxen to pull it when loaded.*

advance, and build up supplies by relaying teams of ox-wagons backwards and forwards. He needed to keep the bulk of the troops in each column together, and hoped that the Zulu warriors, armed with their primitive weapons, would attack the steady lines of British infantrymen, armed with the man-stopping Martini-Henry breach-loading rifle, capable of firing twelve rounds every minute. Faced with this sustained fire, he hoped that the morale of the Zulu *impis* could be smashed, and he could then end the war by capturing the king. He estimated that the campaign would take about six weeks.

The thump of drums filled the air as the 24th Regt began to move northwards from Pietermaritzburg, at the start of their 125 mile march through the wilderness. The Regimental band strained to the tune of 'Warwickshire Lads', as they reached Greytown. One company of the 2nd Bn was left to garrison the town, as they moved up to the little frontier outpost of Helpmekaar, where the column began to take shape.

Two companies of the 1st Bn were temporarily to garrison the outpost, which left thirteen companies of the 24th Regt to proceed to the border. Lord Chelmsford had received no cavalry units from England, so they formed a squadron of a hundred mounted infantry from the various Imperial companies. The mounted volunteers were made up of The Royal Natal Carbineers – who were not issued with carbines – The Newcastle Mounted Rifles and The Buffalo Border Guard. The Natal Mounted Police, under Major John Dartnell, had been on the border since November. Twenty-five recruits had come out from England in August 1878, and their strength was now two hundred. But because of a mishap with their horses they joined the column late. 'N' Battery, 5th Brigade, Royal Artillery, under Lt-Col Arthur Harness, had six 7-pounder field guns. The engineering work would be in the hands of Lt Nolan, and his ten men of the Natal Pioneers, who were joined later by Lt Francis McDowell with four Royal Engineer sappers. The 3rd Regt of the Natal Native Contingent was divided into two battalions. The 1st Bn was commanded by George Hamilton-Browne, and overall command was given to Rupert Lonsdale. Each Company was under European officers. The native troops wore a red rag around their heads, to distinguish them from Zulu warriors. They were badly trained and sullen. Neither the Imperial soldiers nor their own officers had any respect for them, and they were

At the start of the British campaign against the Zulu in January 1879, a typical bustling column of troops, wagons and ox-teams pushes on through broken country along one of the few tracks that were capable of carrying such a convoy.

known to be afraid of Zulu *assegais*. The total strength of the column was 1,700 regulars, 250 mounted volunteers, and 2,500 Natal natives. The transport consisted of 220 wagons, 82 carts, 1,500 oxen, and 70 mules. There was an English journalist with the column. His name was Charles Norris-Newman, or 'Noggs' as he was known. He was special correspondent to the London Evening Standard. There was also several colonial contractors. One of these was a large, rowdy man called Robert Hall, who was to provide bullocks for meat rations among the colonial troops.

On the 9th January the column moved twelve miles due east, across rolling lowlands, and skirting

The Rev George Smith came from East Anglia, and was stationed at St John's Parish, Estcourt. He was well known in the area. This sketch of him dressed in an alpaca frock was drawn by Lt John North Crealock, Lord Chelmsford's military secretary.

the terraced mountains towards the frontier. As the track came over a high ridge and sloped down to the river, it passed a five-hundred feet high mountain known as the 'Itchian' or 'Eyebrow', to the local natives, a quarter of a mile before it reached the Buffalo. On a ledge between the mountain and the track stood two thatched buildings and a cattle kraal, all built mainly of stone. They were the property of a Swedish missionary called Otto Witt, who lived there with his wife and three young children.

Witt had been in South Africa for three years, two of which he had spent learning to speak Zulu. The original owner of the land had been an Irish farmer and trader called James Rorke, who had died about four years earlier. Witt had built the kraal, and had personally re-named the mountain 'The Oskarberg' after the king of Norway and Sweden. He had turned the larger of the two buildings into a school chapel, where he taught the local natives a basic education and the Christian faith.

However, the army had commandeered the homestead, and he had sent his family to the Gordon Memorial mission-house at Umsinga, about twenty miles away across the border. He had stayed behind to keep an eye on his property, and intended to make himself useful by acting as an interpreter between the medical men and their kaffir orderlies. He was joined by George Smith,[1] a tall English missionary, who sported a great red beard. He was vicar of Estcourt mission, but he had been appointed acting chaplain to the volunteers. Most of the natives had gone to Umsinga, but as the once peaceful location began to bustle with activity, a tall copper-coloured teenager watched in awe as the red soldiers came in. His name was Umkwelnantaba – a direct cousin of the Zulu king.

The ponts at the crossing of the Buffalo River at Rorke's Drift in 1879, showing the engineer's tent on the right. It was at this place that the main column of British troops crossed into Zululand on the 11th January, and the Zulu War began.

The Buffalo river at Rorke's Drift is wide. But there is an island about half-way across. It is dangerous and rocky in some places, and the recent heavy rains had swollen it, making the current strong and treacherous. Jim Rorke had cut the banks away to make it safer for transport, and the engineers began to assemble two ponts for the crossing. One was a raft on big barrels, and the other was a pontoon supported on boats. These floating bridges were large enough to carry one Cape wagon, or about eighty men at a time.

Officers bellowed their orders, as detachments of troops came in and pitched their bell-tents. And drivers yelled and cracked their whips as the heavily laden ox-wagons rumbled back and forth. A sprawling military camp was quickly built up around the mission-station.

At that time the Commissariat and Transport Department, although they were considered to be civilians, actually officered by men of the Army Service Corps. Assistant Commissariat Officer Walter Dunne[2] had served in the 9th Frontier War, and had been involved in the operations against Sekukuni, but after an exhausting ride of a hundred miles from the Transvaal to Helpmekaar, he had moved up to Rorke's Drift to form a supply depot in the chapel building. It measured 80 feet by 20 feet, and he supervised the men who began the arduous task of stocking it with stores.

There were 200lb bags of corn, or mealie, wooden boxes filled with biscuits, each weighing a hundredweight, smaller wooden boxes containing 2lb tins of corned beef and wooden ammunition boxes, each containing sixty packets of ten cartridges.

Mr Dunne was joined by Acting Assistant Commissariat Officer James Dalton,[3] a tall red-haired veteran of a line regiment, who was now in his mid-forties. He had served as a volunteer in the recent frontier war, and had been mentioned in despatches for his efficient conduct as the only Commissariat Officer at Ibeka depot. He had volunteered his services for the Zulu campaign. He and Acting Storekeeper Louis Byrne, a young clerk who had been working in Pietermaritzburg, had both ridden up from the capital in torrential rain on New Year's

Day. Second Cpl Francis Attwood[4] of the ASC, had also been working as a clerk in the capital since his arrival in Natal in the previous November. But he disliked the job, and decided to join the column. Five other ASC men were with the column, but they were to move into Zululand with the troops. Some of the regular soldiers who were not fit for the task ahead would also be assigned to store duties as soon as they had organised their tents. There was also a detachment of about three hundred Natal natives, under Capt William Stephenson, 2nd/3rd NNC, who could speak Bantu, that had been attached to the ASC on fatigue duty and would stay behind when the column advanced. One company of regular soldiers would also be left behind to guard the store.

The medical teams and ambulance wagons then came in. The ambulances were ordinary Cape wagons that had been fitted with a sprung frame, which acted as a kind of suspension, to make it more comfortable for casualties in transit. As the native levies began to unload the pack wallets and tentage from the mules, Surgeon-Major Peter Shephard and Surgeon James Reynolds,[5] eyed Witt's thirty year old ramshackle house, that they and the men of the Army Hospital Corps would have to utilise as a field hospital. One Surgeon, two stretcher-bearers, and an ambulance man were assigned to each company, so Doctor Reynolds, and three men of the AHC would stay behind with the company that was to garrison the depot. Reynolds was an Irishman who had much experience of military operations in South Africa. He had served alongside the 1st/24th Regt at Griqualand in 1875, and during the Frontier War he was again with them at Impetu, when the force that was guarding the drift there was besieged by Gcaleka rebels for months.

The house measured 60 feet by 18 feet, and into it Rorke had somehow squeezed eleven poky compartments that were separated by thin partitions made from mud and bricks with slight wooden doors. Doctor Reynolds decided to use one of the rooms to store medical supplies and stretchers, and two front rooms were prepared as casualty stations.

A company of the 99th (Lanarkshire) Regt, attached to Col Pearson's column, make the first crossing of the lower Tugela River. Scenes like this became common at points along the river as the British army went to war.

A close-up of the building which in turn had been Jim Rorke's barn, Otto Witt's chapel, and the British commissariat store. On the verandah Surgeon Reynolds established a temporary casualty station after the hospital building had been evacuated.

His patients would have to be crammed into seven dismal rooms that stretched in an 'L' shape at the western end, and along the back of the building, the doors of which faced south towards the Oskarberg. Only one of the rooms had access to the interior, which meant that the doctor would have to walk around the outside of the building to attend to most of his patients. The beds were straw-stuffed mattresses on hard boards placed on bricks to elevate them off the dusty floor. Reynolds was also responsible for a water-barrel on a cart and several appliances for filtering water. The two buildings were forty paces apart, and each had a verandah facing south, away from the mountain.

No reply to the ultimatum had been received from Cetshwayo when the period of grace expired. So early in the morning of Saturday, 11th January 1879, hostilities began when British troops crossed the frontier into Zululand. Zulu scouts watched from the hills as the barrel raft, platform pont, and a few small boats began to bring the red-coated soldiers across the mist-shrouded river. The mounted men and the natives crossed lower down. The kaffirs linked hands and charged into the water, wading neck deep through the current. Many were swept away and smashed to death on the rocks or

A view of Rorke's Drift post after the defence, looking towards the Oskarberg from the north-west. A more permanent loopholed stone wall has been erected. The storehouse with bare rafters can be seen, and where the hospital stood on the left of the tree.

simply lost their footing and disappeared from the surface. How many died was not known because nobody had bothered to count exactly how many there were to begin with.

Once across and supported by the six field guns, they formed a bridgehead and camp in enemy territory. The troop crossing was completed by 06.30hrs. Progress was halted however, when it was found that the track beyond the new camp was impassable for transport. Lt McDowell and his unit were instructed to prepare the bed for a road across the swampy Bashee River Valley.

The eighty-two men of 'B' Company, 2nd/24th Regt, were the unit left behind to garrison the depot. They were commanded by a stocky, thirty-three-year-old lieutenant, Gonville Bromhead,[6] who had twelve years of service behind him and had come from a distinguished military family. But his own career had been hindered by a serious hearing problem. Some of the disgruntled men of 'B' Company were apt to blame their officer's deafness for the reason why they were regularly given such secondary tasks as guarding supply dumps. Lt Bromhead had asked for permission to fortify Rorke's Drift, but this had been put off. The 4th (King's Own Royal) Regt, and the 5th Company of Royal Engineers were moving up to the frontier, and the job was to be left to them. 'B' Company hoped to rejoin the main advance when these reinforcements arrived.

Sub-Lt Thomas Griffith, 2nd/24th Regt, had been put in charge of the four soldiers of the 1st Bn, who were assigned to store duties. They were Sgt Edward Wilson and Ptes Thomas Payton; Patrick Desmond, a notorious drunkard; and Henry Turner, who suffered from epilepsy. They were acting as issuers of stores. Six more men of the 1st Bn were in the hospital. Pte John Waters was special orderly to Surgeon Reynolds. Ptes Thomas Beckett, William Horrigan, James Jenkins, Edward Nicholson and William Roy, a malaria victim who was also having severe eye problems, were all patients.

There were already more than thirty patients in the hospital. In all twenty-two were soldiers of the 24th Regt. Of the seventeen men from the 2nd Bn, Pte Edward Savage had injured his knee. The rest were from other companies, including Pte John Connolly, 'C' Company, who had a dislocated left knee and Sgt Robert Maxfield, 'G' Company, who was tossing and turning with fever in the Witt's bed. Gunner Arthur Howard of the Royal Artillery had been Col Harness's servant, but he had been left behind in the hospital suffering with diarrhoea. Apparently he was holed up in a corner room near the toilet, along with Gunner Abraham Evans, who

A leather service belt and ammunition pouch of the type used by the 24th Regiment at the time of the Zulu War. The pouch held four paper packets each containing ten rounds of ammunition.

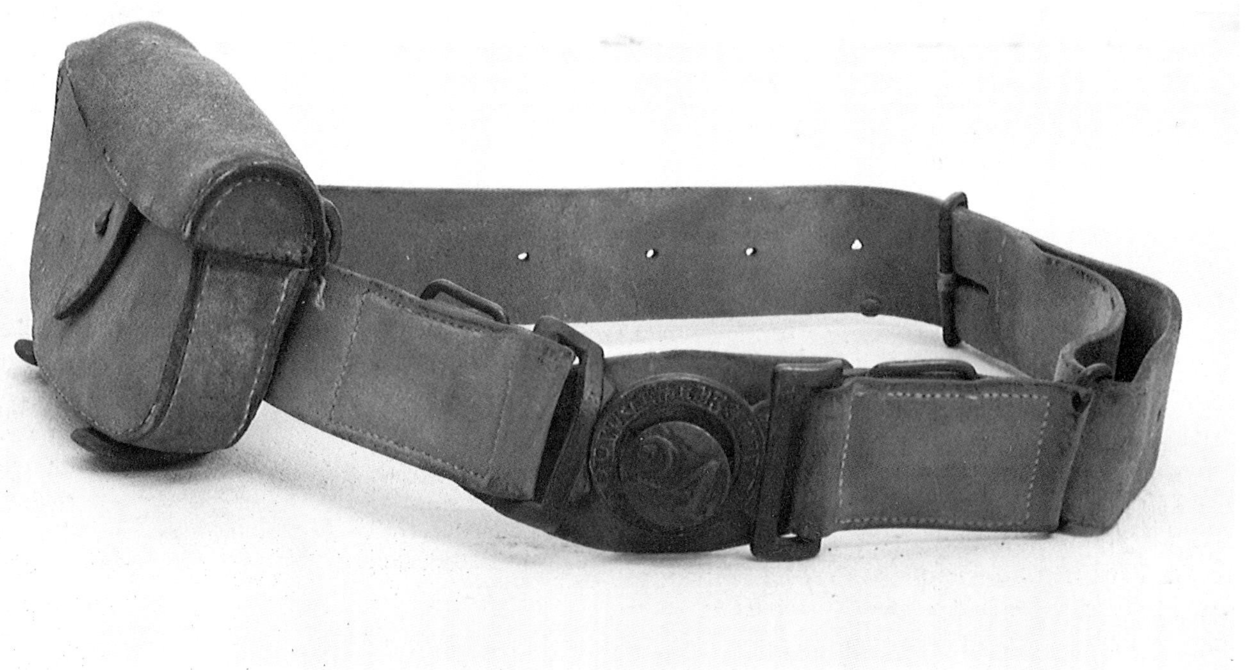

Otto Witt's mission-station was one of several dotted about the landscape of Natal and Zululand, where European church workers preached the gospel. Witt had made himself unpopular locally because of the exaggerated stories he told to the press.

was suffering from a similar complaint. Bombardier Thomas Lewis had been injured in a wagon accident. His thigh, and all down one leg was swollen. Troopers Robert Green and Sydney Hunter of the Natal Mounted Police[7] were stricken with rheumatic fever. And there were five Corporals of the Natal Native Contingent. Friedrich Schiess,[8] a well-built young Swiss, had arrived in South Africa in 1876. Since then his size had helped him to get work as an unskilled labourer. He had fought in the Frontier War with distinction, before joining the 2nd/3rd Regt, NNC. But he had a severely blistered foot from wearing damp ill-fitting boots. The other NCO's were Michael Anderson, William Doughty, Carl Scammel and John Wilson. Cpl James Graham of the 90th (Perthshire) Light Infantry was also invalided. All the bowel disorders had been caused by drinking bad water.

Sihayo's kraal was close to the Bashee Valley, so, on the second day of the invasion, a force was detached to attack his strong-hold in a rocky gorge. Sihayo was at Ulundi, but some of his sons were present. His retainers put up some resistance, but after a short skirmish, thirty had been killed, including two of the chief's sons, and over a thousand head of livestock were in British hands. There were also sixteen Natal Native Contingent casualties. Two natives had been killed and an ambulance wagon brought some of the wounded back to Rorke's Drift. Among them were Lt Thomas Purvis, 1st/3rd NNC, who had received a severe wound when a Zulu bullet went through his arm, and Cpl Jessy Mayer of the same unit, who had been caught below the knee with an *assegai*. Among

the six badly wounded natives was a warrior of Mkungu's Xhosa tribe, of Weenen County, whose thigh had been split by a rifle bullet.

After the engagement, Trooper Henry Lugg of the Mounted Police, a teenager from Devon, was ordered to ride to Pietermaritzburg with despatches. He was eager not to miss the advance into Zululand, so he made a pony express-style ride, using ten horses in relays, and was back at the mission-station by the seventeenth. But his effort was in vain. As he tried to cross the river to re-join his troop, his mount lost its footing, and crushed his knee as it fell. His admission into the hospital brought the number of men on the sick list to thirty-six.

A civilian ferryman named Daniels was looking after the ox-teams at the drift. And Sgt Frederick Milne, 2nd/3rd Regt, (The Buffs), was supervising the ponts. Because of neglected maintenance and constant usage, one of the ponts had been put out of action. Lord Chelmsford was becoming agitated at the slow progress at the crossing, and the engineers were still busy with making good the road. So he ordered another advance party of Royal Engineers to move up to the river to work on the idle pont. Because the rains had drenched the tracks, the movement of wagons was slow, and so it wasn't until the morning of Sunday, 19th January, that a light mule-wagon carrying the necessary equipment, rattled by the mission-station and down to the river. With it came a dark-bearded lieutenant called John Chard,[9] his driver and batman Edward Robson, a corporal and three sappers. Chard was a thirty-one-year-old West Country man, who had passed out at Woolwich eleven years earlier. Most of his service to date had been in southern England, and he had not yet seen action. He was feeling under the weather. His re-vaccination at Capetown had become inflamed, and his right shoulder and side were sore. They pitched their tents by the river, and the sappers set to the task of securing the rope cables that were pulled to move the points across the water.

Above: *Off Duty: The soldiers in camp normally spent their leisure time playing cards or relaxing with their pipes and tobacco. The officers occasionally went hunting for wild game. Here John Chard, wearing his medal, poses for a photograph with fellow Royal Engineers.*

Left: *Lt John Rouse Merriott Chard of the Corps of Royal Engineers was born near Plymouth in 1847. He had only recently arrived in South Africa and had no time to acclimatise when he received orders to proceed to Rorke's Drift.*

Lord Chelmsford had chosen Isipezi Hill, twenty-two miles into Zululand, as the place where the first of the main fortified camps would be constructed, and a reconnaissance party had selected a site for an intermediate, temporary camp, at the base of an isolated hill called Isandhlwana, ten miles away. The road was finally ready on Monday, 20th January, so the column broke camp by the river and a general advance was made towards Isandhlwana. The men of 'B' Company were disappointed not to be going with them, as they wished 'Good Luck' to their friends when they left. As the post settled down, it seemed detached and quiet after the events of the past ten days.

Colonel Durnford was not happy with his command over a reserve force, and Lord Chelmsford was aware of it. So when the British commander received a message from Durnford stating that he had heard a rumour that a Zulu impi was going to attack Natal by way of the Middle Drift, and he was preparing his troops to cross the frontier to meet it, Chelmsford sent a note back at once, ordering him to bring half his force to Rorke's Drift, with the threat that he would be relieved of his command if he did not obey. So during the dark hours of Tuesday morning, Durnford arrived with a strong force of colonial troops, a Royal Artillery rocket battery and a number of wagons, and took over the area that the field column had vacated.

He had 255 mounted volunteers with him, which represented the best troops the colony could offer. Lts Roberts, Charles Raw, and Richard Vause commanded fifty Ngwane natives each. They were known collectively as Sikali's Native Horse. Lt Alfred Henderson led the Hlubi troop of fifty-five BaSotho, and Lt Nathaniel Newnham-Davis of the 3rd Buffs, had the Edendale troop of fifty Kholwa natives. The soldiers in the rocket battery were drawn from the 24th Regiment.

As a temporary appointment, Major Henry Spalding DAQMG of the 104th (Bengali) Regiment, who was one of Lord Chelmsford's staff officers, had been left in charge of the area of Rorke's Drift – Helpmekaar. 'D' Company, 1st/24th Regiment, under Capt Thomas Rainforth, had been requested to move up from Helpmekaar, to form a guard over the drift. But they had not yet arrived. That afternoon Lt Chard received orders from Isandhlwana, stating that his men were to move up to the base camp. So he went to the mission-station to report this to Major Spalding.

Above: *Colonel Durnford, Royal Engineers, was a forty-eight-year-old Irishman. He had been in South Africa since 1871, during which time he had learnt to respect the Zulu and knew them well. However, he had a habit of making decisions that were contrary to his orders.*

Right: *Lord Chelmsford's Orders of the Day, which included the command that Colonel Durnford should move his troops from the Middle Drift to Rorke's Drift, and take up a position on the Zululand side of the river. The column moved on into Zululand the next day, and Durnford's contingent arrived at Rorke's Drift during the early hours of the 21 January.*

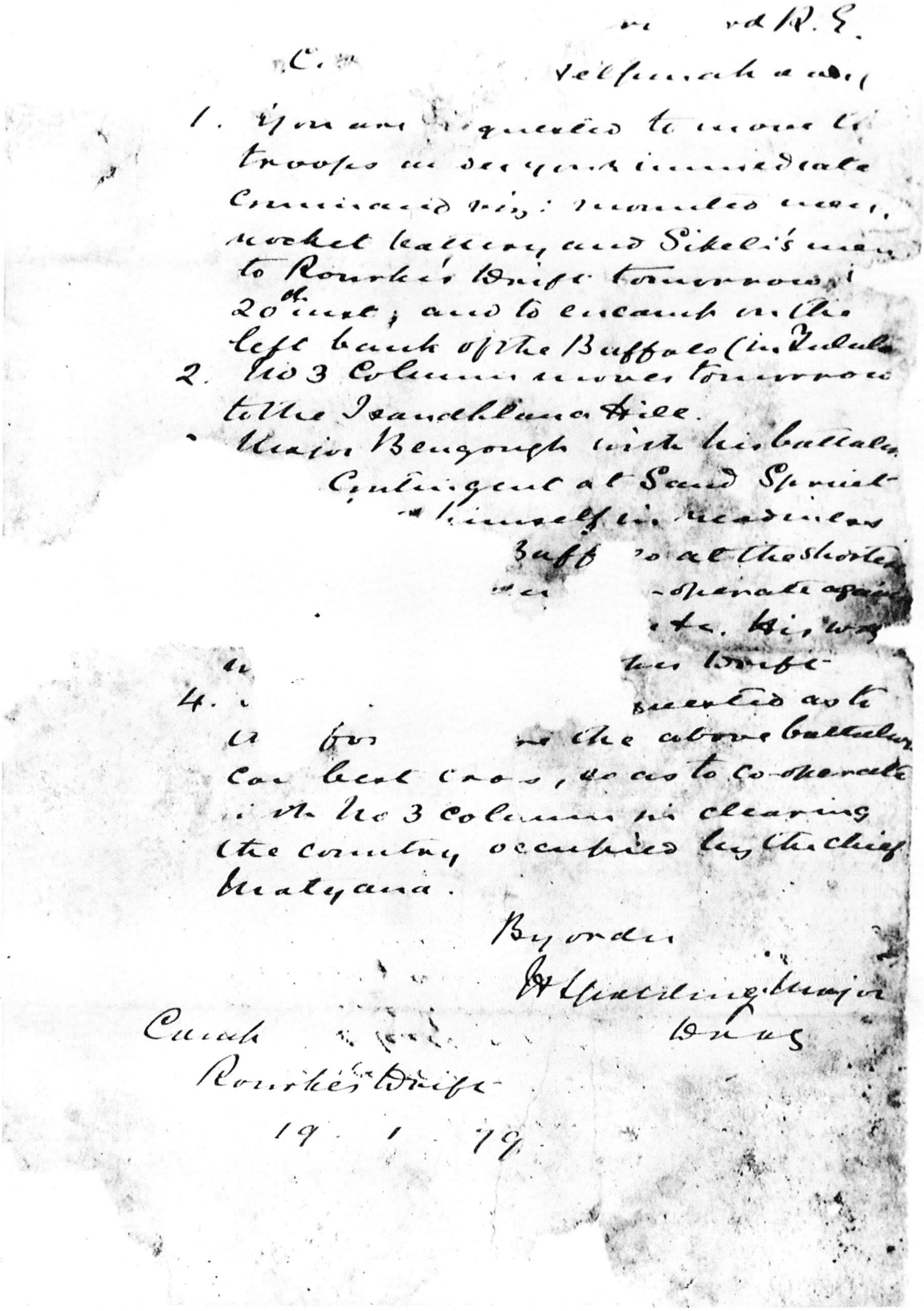
... rd R.E.

C. ... Helpmekaar

1. You are requested to move the troops under your immediate command viz: mounted men, rocket battery, and Sikali's men to Rorke's Drift tomorrow 20th inst; and to encamp on the left bank of the Buffalo (in Zululand)
2. No 3 Column moves tomorrow to the Isandhlwana Hill.

Major Bengough with his battalion ... Contingent at Sand Spruit ... himself in readiness ... Buff... at the shortest ... operate again ... etc. His w... ... Drift

4. ... requested as to ... the above battalion can best cross, so as to co-operate with No 3 Column in clearing the country occupied by the chief Matyana.

By order

J N Crealock Major

Camp ... Drng

Rorke's Drift

19 . 1 . 79

Left: *Lord Chelmsford was an ex-Grenadier Guardsman, aged 51. He had seen service in the Crimea and in the latter stages of the Indian Mutiny. His administrative skills earned him the reputation of an officer with 'great ability and untiring energy.'*

Chard was uncertain about the orders, because they did not seem to include him. So Spalding granted him permission to go to the camp at Isandhlwana to check the orders for himself. Spalding however told Chard that he must postpone the visit until morning, because he first wanted him to select a good place where the Company from Helpmekaar could entrench when they arrived to protect the ponts.

As the light was beginning to fade and the post was settling down for the night, Sub-Lt Griffith arrived at the drift and requested to be ferried across. He was finding his store duties tedious and had decided to ride out to Isandhlwana in search of more exciting activity.

Even before the invasion had started, thousands of Zulus had converged on the main military kraal at Nodwengu, near Ulundi, to take part in an annual cleansing ceremony, called the *umKhosi*, the 'first fruits' ritual. For this the participants wore their war regalia, and therefore many of Cetshwayo's regiments were already prepared for military operations. Those who had remained in their kraals in readiness for the coming harvest, were told that they might soon be needed, and would have to postpone the work, or the task be taken up by the women.

But by the time the camp was forming at Isandhlwana the entire Zulu nation capable of bearing arms had assembled before the King. On Cetshwayo's instructions many of the warriors had brought cattle to exchange for firearms. When news of the British advance reached the capital, the *impis* grew impatient for action. But many of Cetshwayo's council did not want war, so he tried to hang on for a settlement. Eventually he could wait no longer. He stressed to his warriors that he had not wished for war, and that the British were the aggressors. His final instructions were that they should advance slowly to save energy, and not to attack fortified places, especially after dark. The regiments demonstrated their loyalty to the king with a cry of 'Usuthu!'. Then they streamed out across the Mahlabathini plain to defend their kingdom from the white invaders.

A sketch of the tall, lanky figure of Lord Chelmsford. The British Commander-in-Chief was a good leader and was popular among his men.

1: ***George Smith – see p124***
2: ***Walter Dunne – see p126***
3: ***James Dalton – see p127***
4: ***Francis Attwood – see p128***
5: ***James Reynolds – see p129***
6: ***Gonville Bromhead – see p130***
7: ***Natal Mounted Police – see p132***
8: ***Friedrich Schiess – see p134***
9: ***John Chard – see p136***

CHAPTER THREE:
'When Suddenly . . .'

'Worry is rust upon the blade.'
Henry Ward Beecher.

A drizzly rain fell during the night, and the morning of Wednesday, 22nd January 1879, was cold, damp and misty. As the camp at Rorke's Drift began to stir, Lt Horace Smith-Dorrien of the 95th (Derbyshire) Regiment, who was in charge of the transport, arrived back at the river from Isandhlwana with a message for Colonel Durnford. Zulus had been sighted ahead of the camp, and Lord Chelmsford had taken more than half his force forward to meet them. Everyone was expecting action soon. Durnford was to advance his troops to reinforce the base camp. However he had set off towards Helpmekaar with the Edendale men, and had to be sent for when the lieutenant delivered the message.

There was some transport business to attend to at the depot, so Smith-Dorrien crossed the river, where Lt Chard and his men having finished breakfast, were squelching about in the heavy mud on the Natal bank, preparing to move up to Isandhlwana. The party of Royal Engineers crossed into Zululand at about 08.00hrs, which was just after Colonel

Zulu chiefs, with total knowledge of their ground, lead their impis *at great speed, though this may be doubted by the warrior on the right whose belly is, no doubt, the result of a main staple diet of maize and a weakness for millet beer.*

Durnford and his troops set off. Smith-Dorrien went to breakfast with Lt Bromhead. He told him what news there was from Isandhlwana and borrowed eleven cartridges and was on his way back to the base camp by 09.00hrs.

The muddy tracks slowed the progress of the wagons, so Chard rode on ahead, and reached Isandhlwana before Durnford. The camp was set out at the eastern base of the mountain, which was an unusual looking flat-topped feature, whose shape resembled a crouching lion. Lt Chard went to the Headquarters tent, and found that his duties at Rorke's Drift were strictly on the Natal side of the river, keeping the ponts in working order, and maintaining the track back to Helpmekaar. Through a field glass he could see groups of Zulus moving about on the distant hills to his left. They moved in a westerly direction, until the slopes of the mountain behind the camp hid them from view. This was the direction of Rorke's Drift, and he became anxious that they might close-in and prevent him from returning, or even attempt to cut off the supply line by attacking the depot. So he set off back. He met Colonel Durnford on the way, who asked him to pass some messages back along his line of troops. Then the engineers' cart came rumbling up. Chard ordered the sappers to walk with Durnford's men, and told Robson to turn the empty wagon around and follow him back to the drift. He then encountered Lt Smith-Dorrien who was riding back to the base camp. Chard arrived at the river just in time for lunch.

There a message from Major Spalding had been left in his tent. It stated that a guard of seven regular soldiers and fifty natives was to be put on the ponts. They would be relieved when the Company – which was two days overdue – arrived from Helpmekaar. Chard rode up to see Major Spalding at the post. He told him what he had seen at Isandhlwana, and although there had been no sign of any Zulus to his right on the return trip, he pointed out that if an *impi* did attack the ponts, it would be impossible to defend them successfully with the troops allocated to him.

Major Spalding acknowleged this and decided to go to Helpmekaar personally, to see what was delaying the reinforcements. He checked the army

A Zulu chief, similar to the one who appeared on the Oskarberg. The headgear and cowtail streamers enabled him to remain well camouflaged in the bush.

On receiving his orders, Lt Chard rode out of the base camp. Soon afterwards Isandhlwana took its place in history, while he returned to Rorke's Drift – and immortality.

list in his tent to see who would be in charge during his absence. Engineering officers were commissioned as lieutenants straight from passing-out at Woolwich. But Bromhead had served as an ensign (2nd lieutenant) for over four years, before becoming a lieutenant. So although Bromhead had entered the army fifteen months before Chard, Chard had been a full lieutenant for more than three years longer, and was therefore the senior officer. Surgeon Reynolds was a non-combatant, and although Captain Stephenson's rank was the highest, he was not eligible to command regular troops because his appointment was only a temporary colonial one. Major Spalding informed Lt Chard of this, and then set off for Helpmekaar, intending to be back before dark.

Chard was not too alarmed at the situation. There was a large force between the depot and the Zulus, and so he ordered no particular precautions taken. He returned to the river, gave out orders to Lance-Sgt Thomas Williams and his detail, and prepared for lunch. The flies were a nuisance when the men were eating, and the day had become humid and hot, so he decided that it would be more comfortable to eat in his tent. After lunch he lit his pipe and decided to write a letter home. He was interrupted by the natives going back to the depot to be relieved, but apart from that he was able to get on with his correspondence.

Colour-Sgt Frank Bourne[1] and his four sergeants were walking in the hills behind the post when they heard the pounding of artillery coming from the direction of Isandhlwana. They could see clouds of smoke, but the mountain was five miles distant and it was difficult to see clearly with the naked eye. The hills also muffled the sound from the men in the post for whom all was normal, as Lt 'Gonny' Broomhead had allowed most of his men to idle near their tents. Some were entertaining themselves in gaming schools, while others were writing letters home. Many men could hardly read or write, and they were waiting for Colour-Sgt Bourne to return, so that he could help them with their spelling.

A few men were going about their duties as usual. Pte Charles Mason was on guard duty. The hills around Rorke's Drift were still, and there was nothing of importance to report. But he was having problems with the flies that kept landing on him and making him itch. Pte Harry Hook[2] was hospital cook that day, and he was at the cookhouse ovens behind the store brewing tea for the sick. Pte Waters was busy with his hospital orderly duties. Pte Frederick Hitch[3], a tall Londoner, was also at the ovens, preparing food for the Company. Lt Bromhead and Mr Dunne were relaxing smoking their pipes under a tarpaulin which they had propped up with tent poles to shield them from the sun.

Otto Witt and Surgeon Reynolds were preparing their horses to pay a visit to a local missionary. But when the Colour-Sgt returned and reported to the post what he had heard, word reached them, and they decided to go up the Oskarberg with Chaplain Smith, hoping to get a better look at what was happening. When they arrived at the summit they were disappointed to find that the slopes of Isandhlwana blocked their view. They heard three more artillery shots at fifteen minute intervals and at about 13.00hrs the sky went dark, as there was a partial

Lt Adendorff and five Non-Commissioned Officers of the Natal Native Contingent were among the defenders when the Zulu offensive began. This NNC officer wears an infantry officer's style patrol jacket and buff, cord riding breeches. The slouch hat has a red rag – or puggree *– around the crown.*

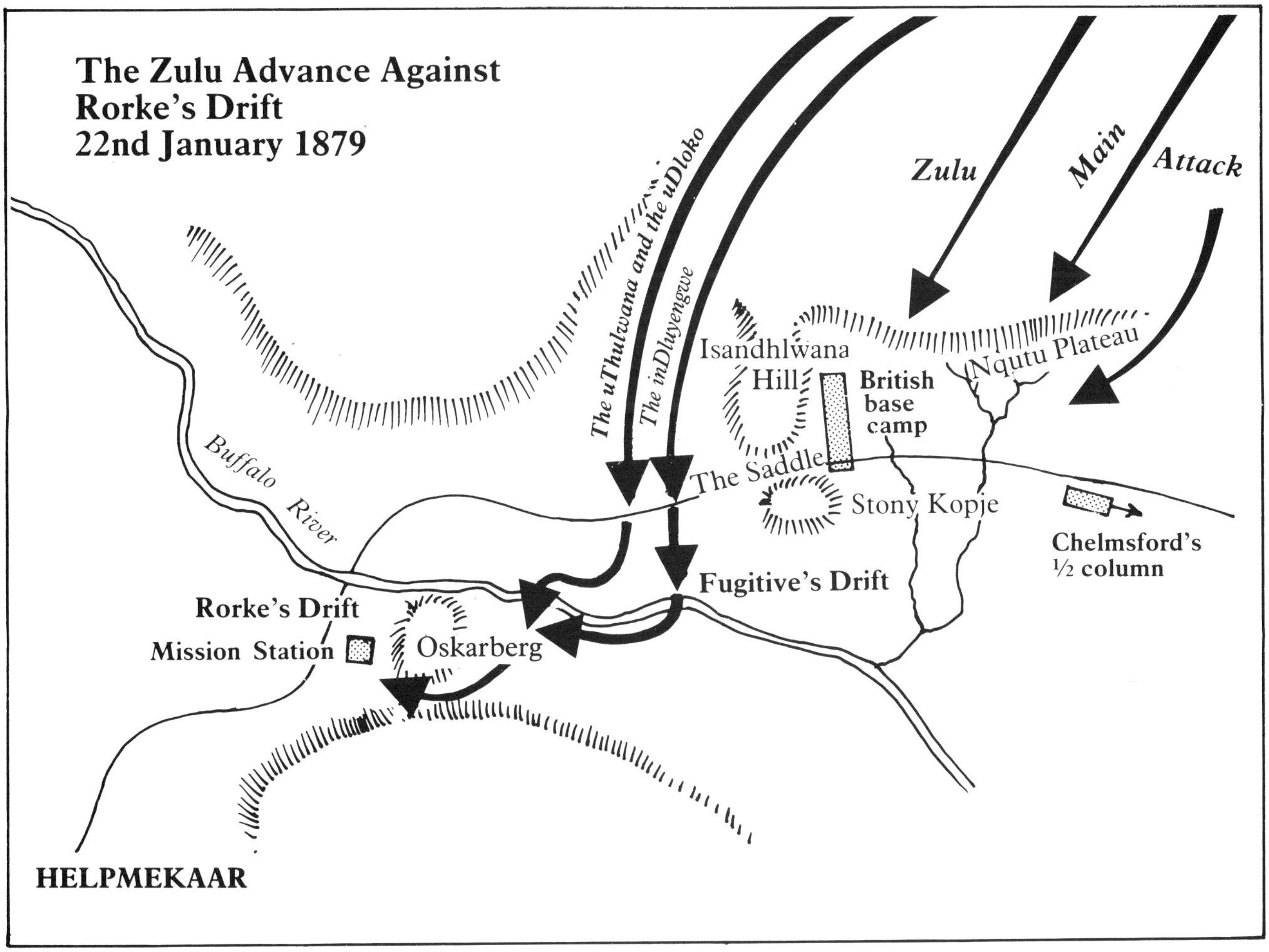

eclipse of the sun. At 13.30hrs a large body of natives could be seen moving around Isandhlwana. They were in good order, and therefore the observers took them to be a detachment of the Natal Native Contingent. They were moving in the direction of Rorke's Drift, but the men on the Oskarberg lost sight of them as they descended into low ground, presumably to search the area for fugitive Zulu warriors.

Just after 15.00hrs Lt Bromhead and Mr Dunne noticed a commotion among the natives across the river. They started to go down to see what the problem was, but they were stopped when Pte Frederick Evans of 'H' Company, who had been attached to the mounted infantry, came galloping into the post. The men in the depot looked at each other apprehensively, suspecting that something was wrong. Evans was in his shirt sleeves and he had no helmet on and he was panic-stricken. They listened with horror as he gasped out the news that the camp at Isandhlwana had been taken by the Zulus and most of the men in it had been wiped out.

They were stunned and the shocking report made it difficult for Lt Bromhead to think straight. But he regained his composure and sent a man down to the river to warn Chard. Nobody could grasp the full significance of the situation at first and they did not know quite what to do.

From the top of the mountain Surgeon Reynolds had seen four colonials riding towards the depot from Isandhlwana on the Natal side of the river. He thought that they might need his assistance, so he rode back down the hill, and got back just as they came pounding into the post. They were visibly frightened, and to Reynolds' surprise, one of them was on Surgeon-Major Shephard's horse. They delivered to Bromhead a pencilled note that had reached them through the combined efforts of three officers who had got out of the camp at Isandhlwana. The note confirmed the previous report, but a look of urgency came onto Bromhead's face when he read that, with the army in disarray, a large Zulu *impi* was at that moment making its way towards Rorke's Drift. This he was to hold at all costs. The fugitives tried to make them realise that the Zulus were in overwhelming numbers, and their only chance was to retreat, which they themselves promptly did, leaving the men to realise the implications of the serious disaster that had happened.

The officers realised the dire position they were in and that there were some quick decisions to be made. There was a feeling among the ranks that the safest thing to do was to try to reach the troops at Helpmekaar.[4] But if they took the decision to retreat, could they get to Helpmekaar before a fast-moving *impi* caught up with them? They had no idea of the size of the *impi*, and they had done nothing to put the post in a state of defence. The depot was open to attack from all sides, and if the Zulus came upon them as it stood, they would not have a chance. But if Lord Chelmsford's advanced force was trying to fight its way back to the river, they could be desperately short of supplies and ammunition. Rorke's Drift depot was their only lifeline. Could they throw up a barricade in time?

When Commissariat Officer Dalton joined them he took the initiative by suggesting without doubt that they should make a defence. He strengthened his opinion by bringing to mind the good supply of building material they had in the store. Mr Dalton and Mr Dunne began to trace a line of fortification as Bromhead ordered the men to fall in. He quickly explained the situation to them, and told them that they were going to stand and fight. If they must die, they would do so with honour.

The tents were pulled down, and the Commissaries, with the help of Sgt Joseph Windridge and the men of the 1st Bn on store duties, began to empty the store of anything that could be used to build a temporary barricade. They piled everything in front of the store, and all ranks worked together to construct the defensive wall and loophole the buildings. There were many young men in the garrison, but they went about the task with efficiency and determination. Even Captain Stephenson's native levies were doing good service. Colour-Sgt Bourne posted look-outs, and selected six men to be posted inside the hospital building to guard the sick as soon as it had been barricaded. He then organised, and took out, a line of skirmishers.

At 15.15hrs, Lt Chard's attention was brought to two men galloping towards the Drift from the east. When they reached the makeshift jetty on the far bank of the river they called out anxiously. Chard could not hear them properly, but he was concerned at their almost hysterical behaviour. He quickly sent the pont across to fetch them. One of them was a Natal Carbineer in his shirt sleeves, and the other was Lt James Adendorff[5] of the 1st/3rd N.N.C. When they reached the Natal bank Adendorff quickly dismounted, took Chard out of earshot of the men and told him that the camp at Isandhlwana was in the hands of the Zulus, with all the men in it massacred. His companion confirmed his report, then rode off to take the news to Helpmekaar. They had left the base camp before any mass rout had begun, and were unaware of the oncoming *impi*.

Lt Chard could hardly believe his ears, but he tried to keep calm and had his horse saddled. He was suggesting to Adendorff that perhaps he had left the scene too early to be sure of what really did happen, when Bromhead's messenger arrived asking him to go up to the post as quickly as possible. He gave orders to load the wagon and prepare the oxen, then posted his men in a good position from where they could watch the ferry, and ordered them to wait until he got back. He then made his best speed up to the mission-station.

He arrived to find the construction of the barricade well under way, and an anxious Bromhead handed him the note. Chard read it, and after learning of the advancing *impi*, had a hurried discussion with the other officers, and agreed with all the decisions that had been taken in his absence. He added his knowledge of field fortification, and the wall was built to include the two buildings and the cattle kraal, while at the same time taking advantage of all the natural defensive features.

The hospital formed the western end of the perimeter. Some of the patients were fit enough to help with the work, and most of the men who were left inside the building were able to use a rifle. Gunner Howard had borrowed Sgt Maxfield's rifle, and Trooper Lugg was hastily tying a piece of strapping around the broken stock of his Swinburn-Henri carbine, preparing to man a loophole in the kitchen extension. The men who were posted to defend the hospital occupied three of the rooms, two of which had access to another. The windows were blocked up with mattresses, and the doors buttressed with mealie-bags and furniture. The interiors were ruined as the men knocked bricks out of the side walls and loopholed the stone end-walls with pickaxes.

A barricade of bags and boxes was begun, to connect the back of the hospital with the front of the storehouse. To save time, two transport wagons were

'Stand and Fight': Sgt Windridge puts his back into it as the men in the garrison are detailed to empty the storehouse of bags, boxes and anything else that could be used to build a defensive wall. The men worked with a sense of urgency, being fully aware that their lives would depend on their efforts to complete the perimeter before the impi *came down on them.*

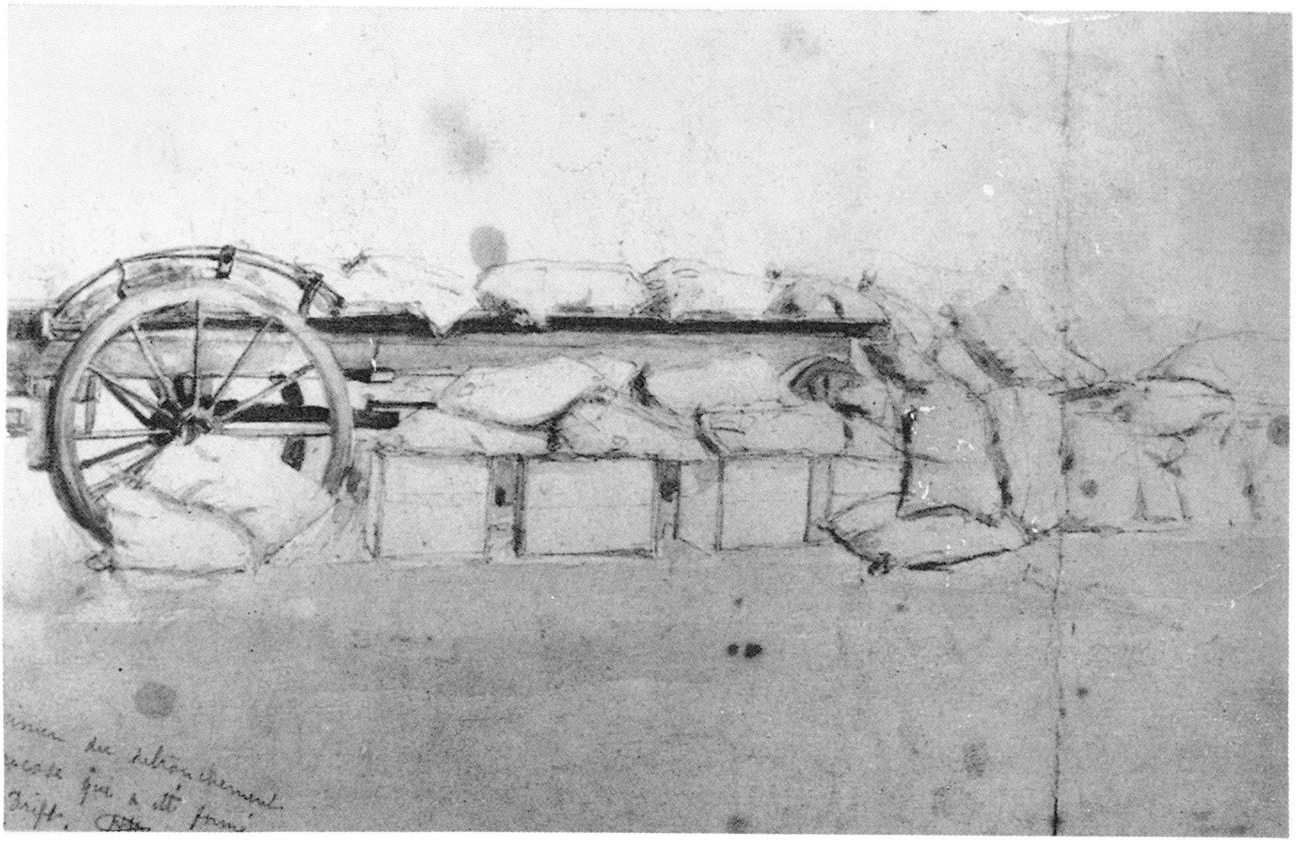

Lt-Col Henry Degacher, who commanded the 2nd Battalion, 24th Regt at the start of the invasion, was a competent artist and drew this detailed picture of one of the wagons incorporated in the south barricade. It was here that the British sharpshooters were posted to keep down the Zulu sniper fire from the Oskarberg.

lifted onto the two-foot wide ledge of rocks that ran a natural course across the front of the post, and were wheeled into place at the store-end of this south barricade. The gaps under the wagons were filled with bags and boxes and bags were piled on top to give extra height and to form embrasures between them through which the men could fire. The high solid back wall of the storehouse completed the south section of the perimeter. Sgt Windridge organised the loopholing and barricading of the gate and windows on the outside of the compound, and men were placed in position to defend them.

The walls of the kraal were only chest high, and were too narrow to stack bags on to gain extra height. But it was very close to the eastern end of the storehouse verandah, and had to be included in the perimeter. The opening between the store and the kraal was filled with mealie bags.

Mealie bags and biscuit boxes were stacked three or more high, all along the top of the ledge, from the north-west corner of the kraal to the western end of the hospital verandah. This formed a breastwork of convenient height to fire over, while at the same time presenting a six feet obstacle to an assailant. However, in front of the verandah the rocky ledge veered outwards, and the rampart continued in a straight line along the top of a slope, before curving inwards to meet the far corner of the building. This left a step that the Zulus could use to get to the same height as the defenders. And there was an area here where only a plank, ten feet long, filled the gap. This place in the northern breastwork was very vulnerable. The length of the improvised wall facing north was over a hundred yards, and the whole perimeter measured about four hundred yards.

When Lt Chard was satisfied that everything was under control he left his fellow officers to supervise the work, and rode back to the river. The fatigue party there was ready to move. The hawsers and cables had been sunk, and the ponts had been moored in midstream. Sgt Milne, Mr Daniels and the detail of men offered to man the ponts and defend them from the decks. This was a gallant request, and Chard was heartened by their courage.

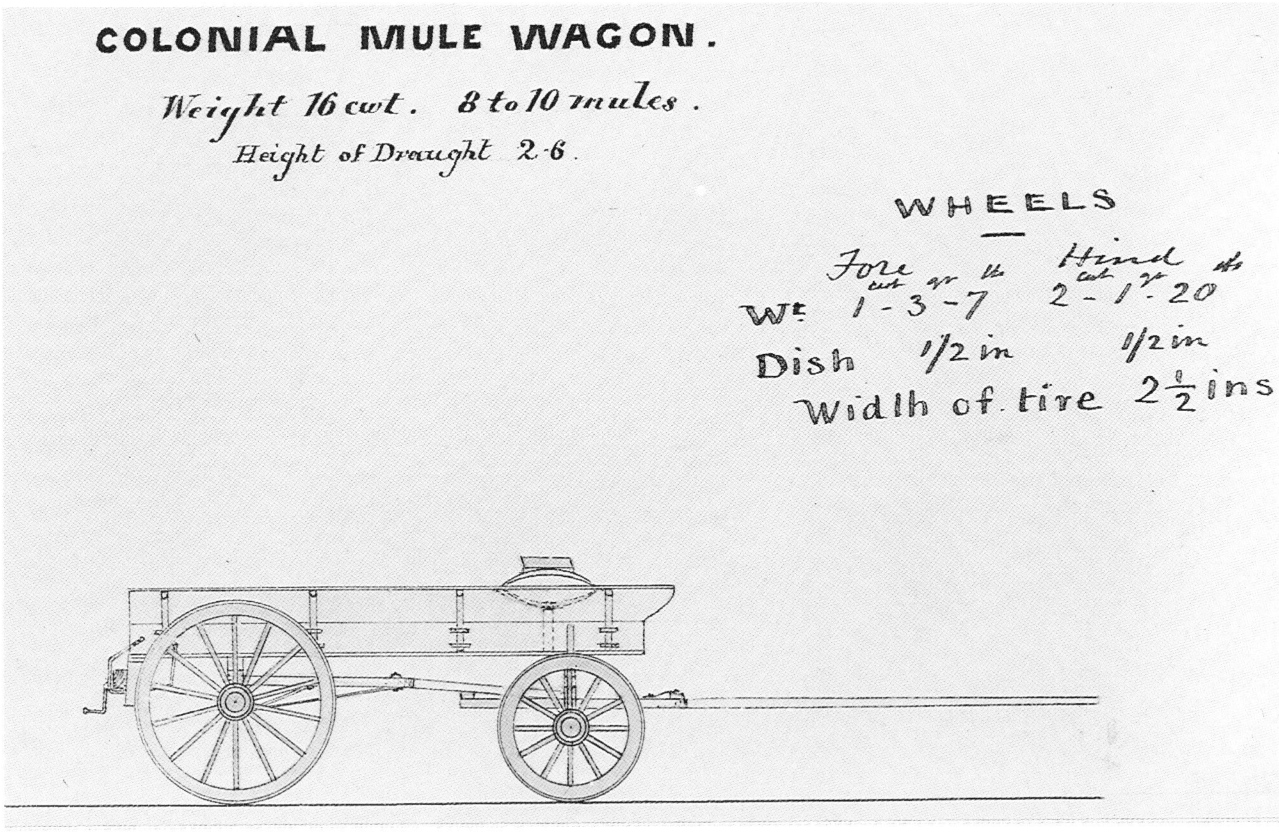

The distance between the commissariat store and the field hospital was about 45 yards, so the inclusion of two colonial mule wagons in the south barricade, each one being twelve feet long, saved the defenders valuable time and energy. The wagons were sturdy, and the gaps below were filled with bags and boxes.

But such an endeavour would be both risky and pointless. They would be better deployed at the post. If the stores depot fell into Zulu hands it would not matter to the column if they destroyed the ferries. They all made their way up to the post.

The fortification was quickly taking shape. Chard went around the fort suggesting improvements, one of which was that the men should make some kind of communication through the hospital building, though this was not done. He also told Sgt Windridge to select a man to guard two casks of rum that were in the store, with strict orders to shoot without question any man who tried to touch them. Windridge ordered Sgt Milne to take up this task.

As the sweating soldiers humped the heavy bags and boxes around, they were all the time wondering, 'How close was the *impi*?' At any moment they might come rushing around the Oskarberg, or screaming up from the river. They might be watching them as they worked, and could attack before they had secured the whole perimeter.

Several more fugitives arrived from Isandhlwana, and the NCOs had to break up little knots of men as they gathered around them to hear their stories. A Natal Carbineer named Fletcher rode by leading a spare horse and Ptes Grant and Johnson of the 1st Bn, who had been with the rocket battery that had that morning gone to reinforce the base camp with Colonel Durnford, came in and made a report. Two mounted policemen named Shannon and Doig also spurred by. As they passed the rear of the hospital they shouted an hysterical warning and rode on. All these men were without their full equipment and their morale had been shattered. They tried to make the men in the garrison realise the danger, and expressed their opinions that they had no chance, before they all galloped on to Helpmekaar. Rorke's Drift was no place for faint hearts, and the garrison was better off without them.

Each time a fresh, gruesome story was told the natives began to mutter to each other in Bantu, and several would then leave the camp in fright. The number remaining to help with the work was dwindling. Then an encouraging reinforcement arrived. Lt Henderson led a mixture of mounted men of the

The Martini-Henry breech-loading rifle was adopted by the British Army in 1871. It was a single-shot weapon, weighing just over nine pounds, and the barrel was nearly three feet in length. If not handled correctly the kick-back was severe enough to break a man's collar bone. It was nevertheless considered the best rifle of its day.

The breech-loading mechanism: The lever behind the trigger guard was depressed to uncover the breech and eject the used cartridge. A fresh round was then inserted in the chamber and raising the lever closed the breech for firing. It fired a .45 bullet, and was most effective at about four hundred yards.

Hlubi and Edendale troops totalling about a hundred men up to the depot. Bob Hall was also with them. Lt Chard asked Henderson to send a detachment down to the river to watch over the Drift, and another to reconnoitre behind the Oskarberg to check the enemy's advance, so as to hold them back as much as possible to give his men more time to finish the fort. When forced to retire, they were to assist in the defence of the store and hospital. Mr Dalton also asked Henderson and Hall to try to rally the edgy kaffirs to stop them from sneaking off until the work was done.

Otto Witt and Chaplain Smith had watched several of the fugitives returning. Although it crossed their minds that the column could be falling back, they were reassured by the fact that none of them were redcoats. Suddenly, they noticed several natives involved in a skirmish around a farm building on the Natal side of the river, at a drift about a mile away. Flames and thick smoke began to rise from an isolated barn. Shortly afterwards, large numbers of natives came into view to their left, moving slowly up from the river. They formed in a mass and squatted down to take snuff. It was another thirty minutes before they rose and continued their advance towards the Oskarberg. The two clerics were deceived by their leisurely approach, but their suspicions were aroused when they saw that they were not wearing the red rag of the Natal Natives. The increasing force was within rifle range before they noticed that the two men on grey horses, who were leading them, were not Europeans. They were struck with terror when they suddenly realised that the oncoming force was a Zulu *impi*. They hastily made their way down the hill.

When they got back they found the garrison already alerted. Witt became angry at the sight of what had been done to his property, and cried out in broken English that he was concerned for his family at Umsinga. So he, Umkwelnantaba, and Lt Purvis, whose arm was too badly injured for him to be of any use, rode away. Chaplain Smith decided that in such a situation the presence of a man of God was never more needed, and so he elected to remain. The departure of Lt Purvis left thirty-five sick men in the camp, of which thirteen were able to assist their comrades at the barricade. This left twenty-two still in the hospital, along with the orderly, Pte Waters and the six men who had been told off to defend the building. Nine of the patients were bed-ridden.

Mr Dalton requested Lt Henderson and Bob Hall to scout beyond the shoulder of the Oskarberg, to check on the mounted men, and to bring back a report on the *impi*. As they rode out towards the hill, the defenders were told to stop work, and the officers saw to it that every man was allocated a position on the perimeter to defend. It was important to give them a breather before the attack began. The hospital water-cart was already within the enclosure, ammunition had been issued, and the opened boxes of reloads had been put in convenient places close to the men. There were two piles of bags in front of the store and stacks of wooden boxes inside.

Lt Chard knew that his weapons were far superior to those carried by the Zulus. Even if they had acquired firearms, good marksmanship was not one of their qualities. He could also gain comfort from the fact that the reputation of bravery attributed to Zulu warriors could be matched by the tradition of coolness and gallantry of the British infantryman. Whether or not they survived depended on the strength of the defences, and how heavily outnumbered they were.

Pte Hitch had been trying to get the tea ready before the Zulus attacked. He had just brought the last of four kettles into the compound, when Lt Bromhead told him to get onto the roof of the storehouse to keep a look-out. This gave him a good vantage point to over-look the area. There were several features around the position that the Zulus could use to their advantage. The heights of the Oskarberg loomed over the post about four hundred yards to the south, while there were some deep *dongas* on the approach from the south-west and from the east towards the river. To the south of the store stood the shed that had been used as a cookhouse, and beside it were two round stone ovens. There were also two shallow drainage ditches, one running away from the store, and the other running, at about twenty paces away, virtually parallel with the wagons in the south barricade. To the south-east the tents of the 24th Regt littered the ground. To the north, thick bushes grew right up to the ledge of rocks, and there had been no time to cut them down. Some thirty paces away from the hospital verandah there was a wall about five feet high, running parallel with the ledge. Just beyond the wall were two tall poplar trees, to which some horses had been tied, while a rutted track ran by on the other side of the wall. Beyond that there was a fenced garden. To the west there was rising ground

and a hay-stack and the toilet stood in this vicinity. To the east the ground sloped down towards the river, where there was an additional rough stone kraal close to the well built one, with the engineers' wagon standing just beyond it.

At about 16.20hrs, the sound of rifle fire could be heard from behind the Oskarberg, and this triggered a mass colonial desertion. The detachment of Durnford's Horse could now be seen retreating towards Helpmekaar. Chard's *vorlooper* lad stole a horse and went with them, while his kaffir wagon driver scampered off to find a cave to hide in on the hill. The hundred or so nervous natives that were left also took to their heels, and Captain Stephenson followed on his horse. Cpl Anderson had left the hospital to fight at the wall, but he lost his nerve and fled after them. The angry men behind the defences called after him to come back, but he ignored them. Tempers flared, and a rifle bullet brought him down.

The number of men in the garrison was by now reduced to 139, all ranks. Of these 104 were fit, but only eighty were combatants. At first they were demoralised by the flight of so many men though it was decided that the reliability of the natives had always been suspect, and it was fortunate that they had shown their weakness before the attack. Chard however now felt that the line of defence was too extended, and therefore ordered the non-combatants to begin the construction of a row of biscuit boxes, extending from the north-west corner of the store to a point about seventy feet away at the northern breastwork. This would provide an entrenchment that would be of great value if the defenders were forced to fall back from the original perimeter.

The sound of pounding hoofs and raised voices then caught everyone's attention. It was Henderson and Hall galloping hell for leather towards the post. As they moved around the position, Henderson reined in and reported that he had not been able to get his men to obey orders. Hall yelled a warning that the Zulus 'as black as hell and as thick as grass'[6] would soon be upon them. They rode around the outside of the post beyond the store, and eventually made off towards Helpmekaar.

It was past 16.30hrs now. Only ninety minutes had elapsed since the calm had been broken at Rorke's Drift. The non-combatants were still working on the second layer of biscuit boxes that would make the reserve defence line waist high. All round there was a clicking noise as the ranks of men in single-breasted red tunics, dark trousers and low-brimmed tropical helmets, fixed their twenty-four inch bayonets to their rifles. The bayonets glistened in the bright sunshine. Some of the men at the perimeter were dismounted colonials, wearing dark corduroy uniforms and the slouch hat.

The feeling of isolation was terrifying, particularly in the face of an as yet unseen enemy, who were about to attack them and would literally try to cut them to pieces. Stories about the Zulus' bloodthirsty atrocities were rife among the colonials, and had been passed on to the British regulars. It would be useless to run because there was no safe refuge. And it was known that the Zulus took no prisoners. Some men made pacts to kill each other when all was lost, to save themselves from the horror of Zulu ritual savagery. Hearts began to pound. They could now only put their faith in their tense and nervous comrades beside them and their trained skills with rifle and bayonet.

Private William Roy, 1st/24th Regiment was a patient in the hospital when news of the Isandhlwana massacre reached the mission-station. He was suffering from malaria, and a disease which was affecting his vision.

1: ***Frank Bourne – see p138***
2: ***Harry Hook – see p140***
3: ***Frederick Hitch – see p144***
4: ***Helpmekaar – see p146***
5: ***James Adendorff – see p147***
6: ***Experiences of Combat – see p148***

CHAPTER FOUR:
'Here they come!'

For how can man die better,
Than facing fearful odds
For the ashes of his fathers
And the temples of his gods.
Thomas Macaulay.

A cry of 'Stand to!' echoed around the post, and as Colour-Sgt Bourne and his skirmishers ran in and took their places at the barricade, all eyes turned to the western flank of the Oskarberg, where about fifty Zulus had come into view. They extended in open order and began cautiously to edge forward, prancing about as they did so. Their intention was to provoke the men in the garrison to open fire, so that the single Zulu who had appeared on the crest of the Oscarberg could count the guns. Nervous fingers began to ease pressure on the triggers, but the warriors were some distance away and again a command rang out, ordering them to hold their fire.

Pte Hitch called down to Lt Bromhead that he could see the main body of the *impi* behind this advance guard, and he caused a flurry of mixed remarks when he estimated their numbers as four

The Zulu impi *plunges into the fast-flowing water and the warriors surge neck-deep across the Buffalo River to the Natal bank. Frustrated at having been held back at Isandhlwana, despite orders, they decided to '. . . go and have a fight at Jim's.'*

thousand or more, their columns stretching right across the pass from the Oskarberg to another hill. He reported that several hundred were preparing for attack, in a long curved line. He could also see scores of warriors creeping along the lower terraces of the Oskarberg, where they were taking cover in caves and settling down behind rocks. These Zulus carried some of the firearms that had been captured from the action at Isandhlwana, and as Hitch took a prone position below the apex of the roof, they exchanged a few shots. Hitch also took a pot shot at the dark coloured figure standing out against the bright blue sky on top of the hill. But his target was out of range.

The reconnoitering Zulu on the Oskarberg then waved a signal, and a stout, mounted inDuna brought forward a mass of warriors about six hundred strong over the rise, and into full view of the post.

These were from the inDluyengwe regiment, known to be about a thousand strong, and comprising unmarried thirty-three-year-olds. Their original inDuna, Usibebu, one of Cetshwayo's fiercest rivals, had been wounded at Isandhlwana. The overall leader of the *impi* that was massing at the Oskarberg was Dabulamanzi, Cetshwayo's ambitious thirty-five-year-old brother. His *impi* had acted mainly as reserves at Isandhlwana, and resenting not having taken any major part in the battle, had been driven on to kwa jimi – 'Jim's Place' – by their desire to prove themselves. Dabulamanzi was fully aware that he was disobeying his royal brother's order not to attack fortified places, and he knew that it would be dark in two hours. But the defenders in the fort seemed very few, and his warriors were spoiling for a fight. He felt sure that he could take the post quickly. Although the new inDuna had not had time to assert his authority, Dabulamanzi decided to give the young regiment the opportunity to wash their spears.

Their war regalia was designed to give them a ferocious appearance. They wore loin cloths with horse-hair fringes and animal tails streaming from their elbows and knees. Many wore cow-tail necklaces and beadwork ornaments. They carried black shields with a white splash and their deadly stabbing *assegais*. A few had rifles. After one loud chant of their war-cry 'Usuthu! Usuthu! Inkomo ka baba!' they bagan to advance at a steady trot. They

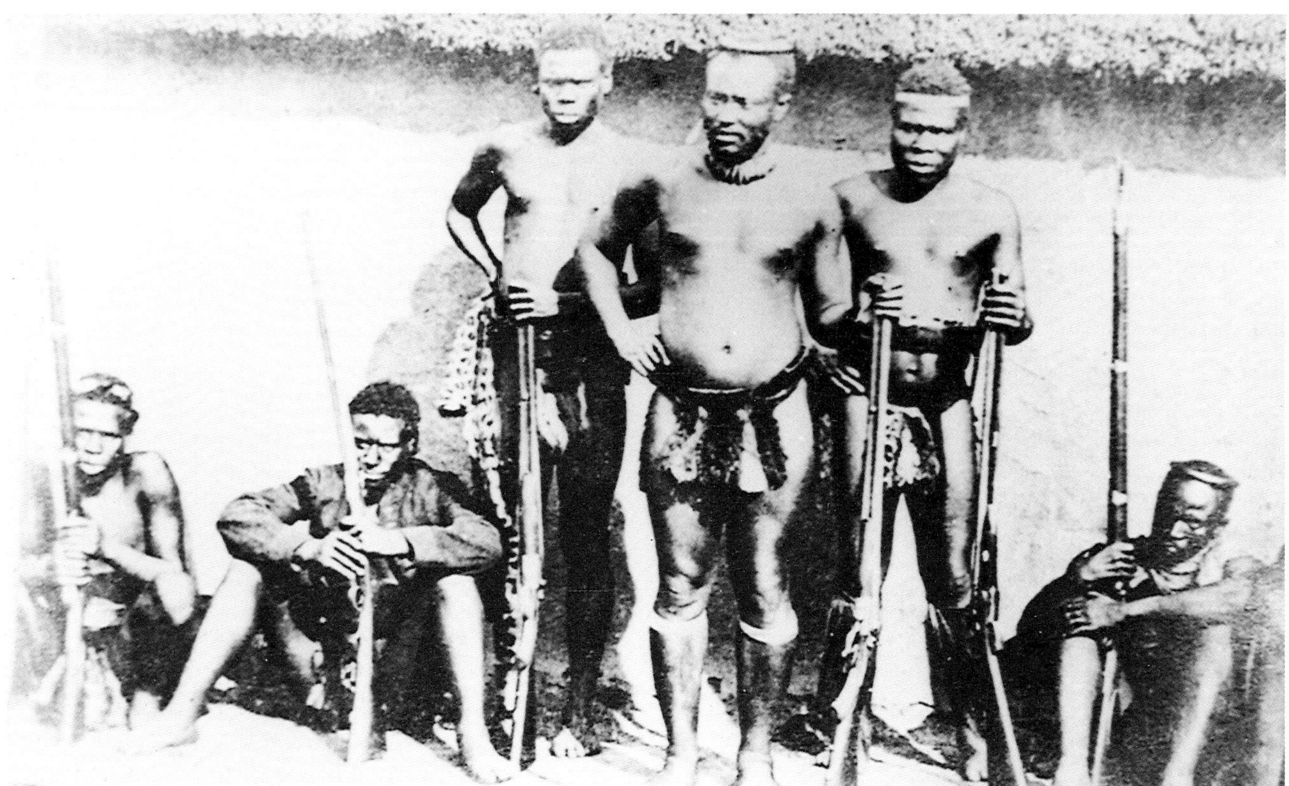

Prince Dabulamanzi, who commanded the Zulus at Rorke's Drift, was Cetshwayo's brother, and was an ambitious man.

Dabulamanzi on horseback. Having made the decision to move swiftly on Rorke's Drift, he expected the battle to be an easy one.

swerved to the right, and without a sound made a mad rush at the south barricade.

At about six hundred yards the defenders' rifles thundered the first volleys and clouds of black smoke rose from the barricade. Chamber levers clicked back, and used cartridge cases tinkled onto the rocky ground. The first shots were wild, but at about four hundred and fifty yards the firing steadied, and a bullet from Pte James Dunbar's rifle brought the inDuna crashing from his horse. The firing quickly gained momentum, and as the lead slugs smashed into the attackers, who were so thick that it was almost impossible to miss, the force of impact lifted them off their feet before they fell, tumbling and rolling, or sprawling over each other. The sight of this gave the soldiers confidence, but their fire was failing to stop them. The warriors in the rear leaped over those who were falling before them, and stooped forward as they ran, trying to make a more difficult target. Their legs made a strange whooshing noise as they pushed through the grass, and regardless of their dreadful losses and the danger to their lives, they raced forward.

The onrush was getting uncomfortably close, and the men behind the wagons and boxes at the south barricade were bracing themselves to receive the coming black tide with their bayonets, when at about fifty paces the Zulus were caught by such heavy volleys from the south barricade and the back of the hospital, together with a tremendous cross-fire from the store that the advance was checked.

Those Zulus who were carrying rifles scattered and took cover around the cook-house and ovens, while others scrambled into ditches and took advantage of anything that would shield them from the bullets. Some ran up to the storehouse and threw themselves against the walls, but there was little cover there and they were shot down. The greater number veered to their left without stopping and rejoined the rear of the main body of the *impi*, which Dabulamanzi was leading in a wide sweep around the hospital. Some then came in to attack the corner of the defences in front of the verandah, while the rest rushed into the thick bushes and trees to the north-west and, under this cover, pushed further around the post.

The warriors who had taken cover in front of the south barricade then opened a desultory fire, and those on the Oskarberg, after waiting to see the outcome of the first attack, sent a barrage of bullets raining down onto the post. Other Zulus had taken cover at the mouth of the cave where Chard's petri-

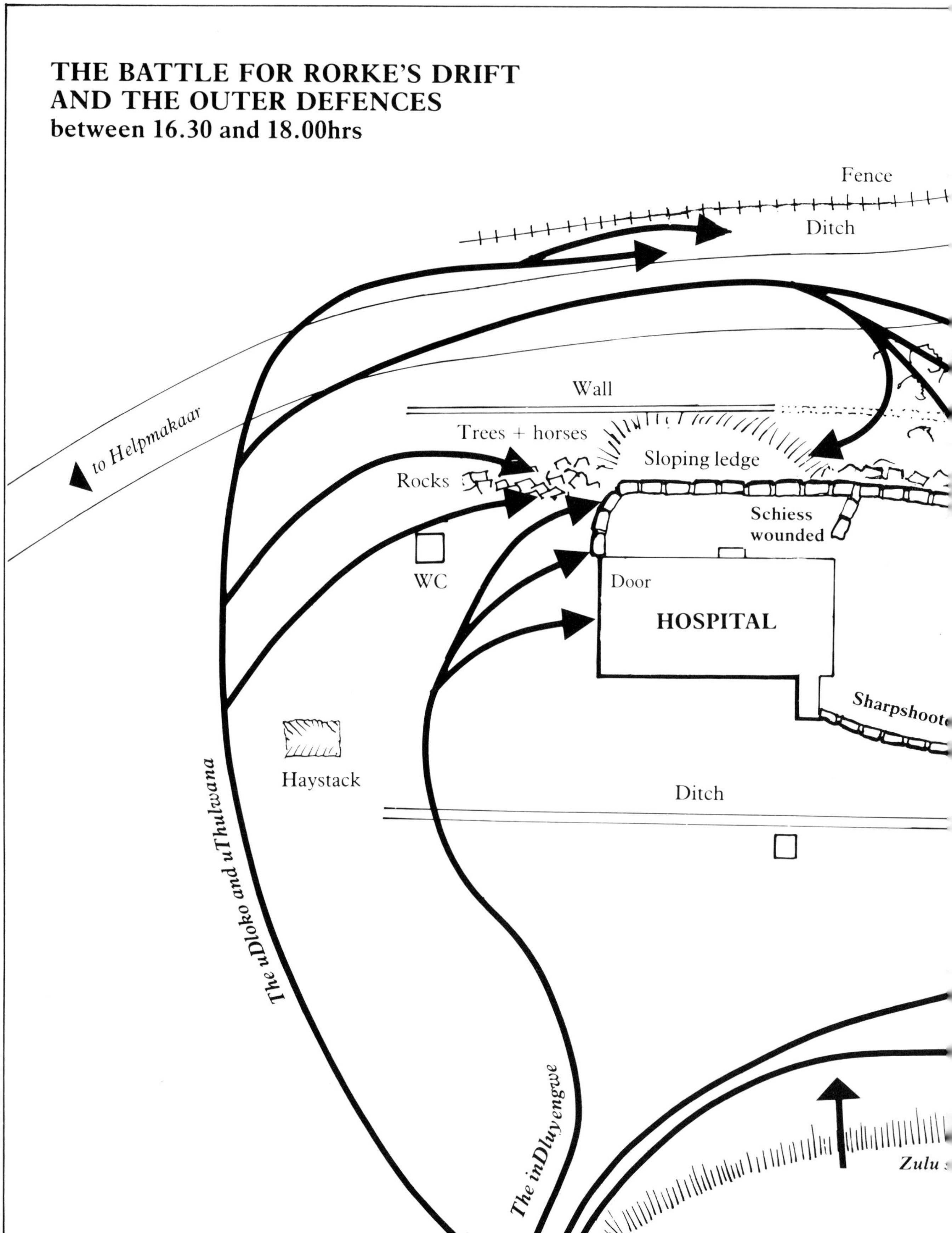
THE BATTLE FOR RORKE'S DRIFT
AND THE OUTER DEFENCES
between 16.30 and 18.00hrs
Fence
Ditch
to Helpmakaar
Wall
Trees + horses
Sloping ledge
Rocks
Schiess
wounded
WC
Door
HOSPITAL
Sharpshoot
Haystack
Ditch
The uDloko and uThulwana
The inDluyengwe
Zulu

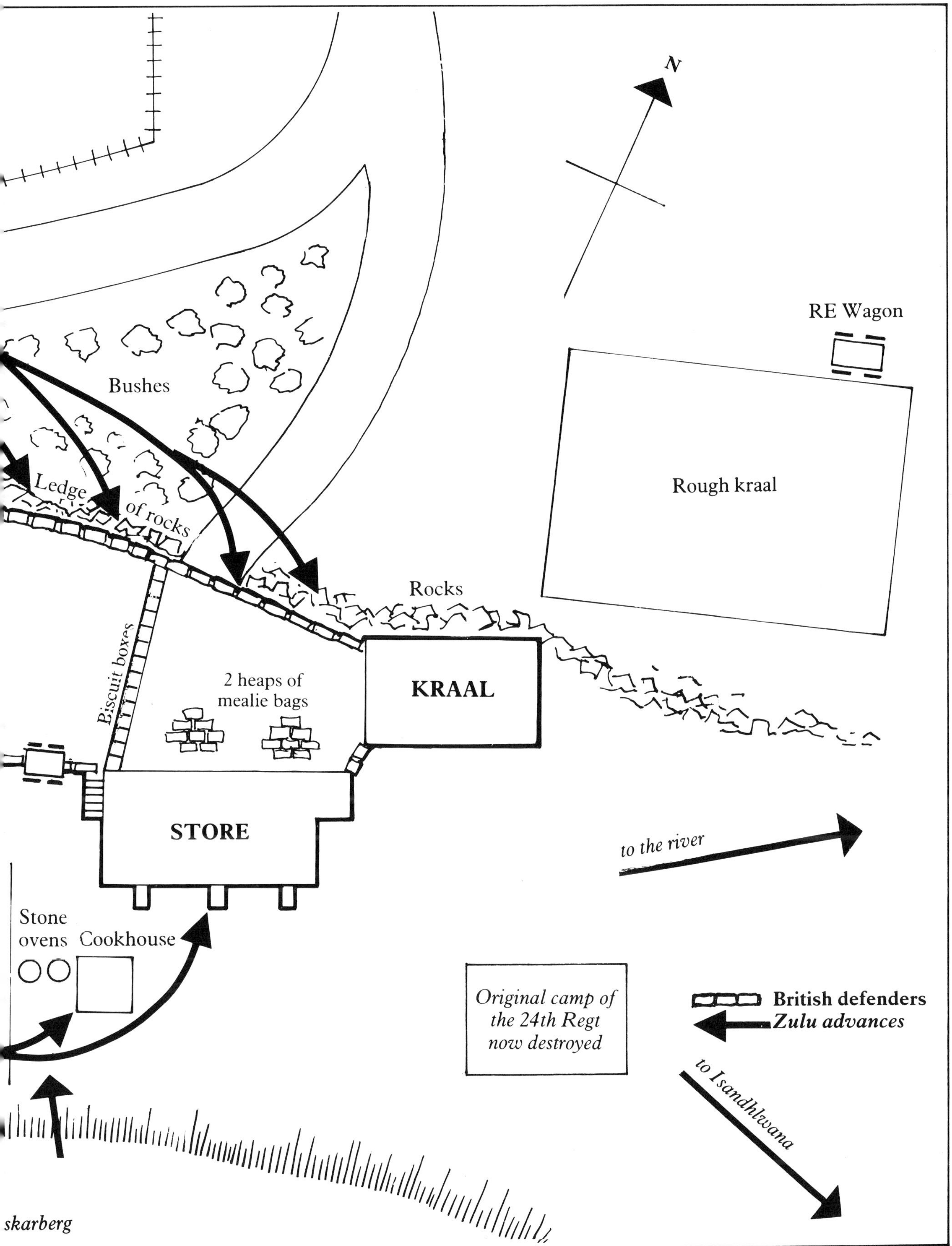
N
RE Wagon
Bushes
Rough kraal
Ledge of rocks
Rocks
Biscuit boxes
2 heaps of
mealie bags
KRAAL
STORE
to the river
Stone
ovens
Cookhouse
Original camp of
the 24th Regt
now destroyed
British defenders
Zulu advances
to Isandhlwana
skarberg

fied wagon driver was hidden in the darkness. Even there they were unsafe, as British rounds came in, and one Zulu was hit.

Pte Hitch slid off the roof of the storehouse, fixed his bayonet as he ran across the compound, and took up a position behind the men in front of the hospital. They gritted their teeth as they met the rush of warriors, and there was the rattle of bayonet on shield, and the clatter of rifle barrel on *assegai*, as the Zulus threw themselves against the breastwork, and with fanatical bravery, tried to get over. There was a desperate struggle as some warriors climbed onto the bags and slashed and stabbed at the defenders in their frenzy, while others dug at the barricades in an attempt to pull them down. The defenders parried, prodded and thrust violently back at them with their bayonets, or blasted them at point blank range. Some warriors fell screaming with dreadful injuries. When necessary the butt of a rifle or even a swift left hook did the job of keeping a warrior out. The officers and non-combatants gave shouts of encouragement and warnings of danger. Some Zulus began to smash their spears on the doors at the western end of the hospital. Others grabbed at the rifle barrels of the men who were shooting at them through the loopholes.

The determined attack was pushing the defenders back from the area in front of the hospital, to a dog-leg breastwork that jutted in from the outer perimeter. Pte Hitch shot a Zulu as he and several other warriors jumped onto the step to get at the soldiers. But before he could reload another warrior broke through, dropped his weapons, and grabbed the muzzle of Hitch's rifle trying to wrench it from him. Hitch had a firm hold of the butt and managed to hold on to it. As they struggled he managed to reload the weapon, and shot the Zulu, who held his grip for a while before falling. Lt Bromhead then lead a counter-charge, which threw back the attackers at bayonet point and gave his men renewed spirit. The tide changed, and the Zulus were forced to scramble back out of the fort, and take refuge in the bushes. But within moments a second wave of warriors attacked the position.

The whole place was now alive with Zulus. The main body had moved around the post, using the thick bushes as cover. Many were crouching behind Witt's wall, and they had also occupied the ditches, the garden and the hollow in which ran the track. The defenders could not see them, but they could hear them, and some fired into the bushes in the hope of scoring an unseen hit. The Zulus crept right

A view of Rorke's Drift post from the Oskarberg, where Zulu snipers were positioned to fire down on the garrison. It was also from this direction that the impi *first attacked the post. The monument and cemetery can be seen in the foreground.*

A young warrior of the inDluyengwe regiment who appeared on the neck of the Oskarberg. The leopardskin headband is the only item of ceremonial dress he has retained. He is carrying the small war shield bearing the colours of an umarried regiment.

up to the ledge of rocks extending as far to their left as the bushes reached, where they surprised the soldiers as they rose up and attacked the breastwork.

These were mostly warriors of the uDloko, about two thousand forty-one-year-olds, and the uThulwana, the regiment that Cetshwayo had once belonged to, which totalled about a thousand forty-five-year-olds. The inDluyengwe and the uThulwana were known collectively as the uNdi Corps.

The men in the garrison did not know at the time, that a fourth regiment called the iNdlondlo had set off towards Rorke's Drift, but they had turned back. Some carried white shields and others ruddy shields with light spots, and most wore the head-

Lt Chard's panoramic sketch of the mission-station and the area around Rorke's Drift post, viewed from the north. Chard has indicated the direction from which the Zulu impi *first appeared. This sketch, and the diagrams in this work, which are based on his official scale plan, should give the reader an accurate picture of the garrison's defences.*

ring of the battle-experienced married regiments. They wore monkey-skin earflaps, plumes of exotic birds such as the crane and ostrich, otterskin headbands and ornaments of beadwork. Snuff boxes dangled from their ear-lobes, and ivory snuff-spoons were fastened to their heads.

Once again the fighting became fierce, as

Bromhead and his men drove them out of the compound near the hospital. Weapons clashed as the Zulus kept one side of the breastwork while the defenders held their ground on the other. Each time the Zulus were driven back into the bushes they would shout their war-cry 'Usuthu', clash their *assegais* against their shields, then spring up and again rush at the breastwork. The defenders replied with defiant shouts, and each onslaught was met with rapid fire. As the defenders stabbed with their bayonets the Zulus grabbed at them and some were wrenched from the rifles. But they were continually driven back into the bushes. There were acts of bravery on both sides, as they were locked in the fierce brutality of war. Cpl Schiess had been strong enough to help at the breastwork, and on several occasions he had climbed over the bags and got amongst the Zulus on the rock step, smashing them off with the butt of his rifle, and thrusting his bayonet at them as they pounced forward and grabbed at him. The men fighting near him were impressed at his bold conduct, and were alarmed when he was shot in the foot of his already injured leg. But it boosted their morale when, after flinching at the initial stab of pain, he simply ignored the wound and kept at his post.

The backs of the men defending this area were completely exposed to the rifle-fire of the Zulus on the Oskarberg terraces. Pte Thomas 'old king' Cole had been one of the men posted inside the hospital, but he ran out of the building to join the men at the breastwork. They were almost immediately showered with his blood and brain tissue, when a Zulu slug went straight through his head, and then hit Pte James Bushe on the bridge of his nose, splattering his face with blood. Pte Nicholson and Pte Roy had left the hospital to help. But Nicholson also had his brains scattered by enemy fire, while Pte William Tasker and several other men were slightly wounded.

Surgeon Reynolds was by them at once, putting cold water on the injury, and applying a cold compress to stop the bleeding. He was looking after a terrier dog called Pip, which belonged to an officer who had moved up with the 3rd Column. The excited animal bounded along at his feet barking at the Zulus. The Rev Smith spent his time moving along the perimeter with his native servant handing out cartridges from his hat, as well as reproving curses and stopping to give spiritual consolation to the wounded. Birds were darting through the smoke overhead, disturbed and confused by the cries and turmoil. Higher in the sky vultures were hovering as they waited in scavenging anticipation.

After some time a cloud of dust could be seen rising from behind the hills on the track from Helpmekaar. Some men said that they had caught a glimpse of red now and then, and they were given new heart when they thought that the two companies of the 1st Bn were coming to their aid. But the dust dispersed and they waited in vain.

The sharp shooters at the south barricade were concentrating their fire power towards the Zulus on the Oskarberg, who were sending bullets whizzing over their heads. Some slugs rattled into the wagons and wooden boxes, thumped into the mealie bags, or went pinging off the walls of the store and hospital. Cpls William Allen[1], Alfred Saxty[2], and John Lyons were among these men, exposing themselves over the barricade to get a more accurate aim. Many warriors were being hit, and Pte Dunbar received a few complimentary remarks when he brought down eight Zulus with as many consecutive shots.

Suddenly there was panic all around when thick smoke began to rise from the far end of the hospital roof. The Zulus had set light to the thatch. Fortunately for the garrison the grass was tightly packed and only smouldered at first. To add to this crisis the soldiers were once again being pushed back from the area in front of the verandah, and the breastwork was beginning to sag inwards from the sheer weight of Zulu numbers.

Surgeon Reynolds and the AHC men realised that they would soon have to abandon the medical supplies. So they had to move quickly to try to save some of them. He and his two privates, Thomas Luddington and Michael McMahon dashed to the dispensary, while his corporal, Robert Miller, and Mr Dalton covered them with their rifles. As they were grabbing as much as they could, a Zulu sprang forward and pulled Cpl Miller towards him by the muzzle of his rifle and was about to thrust his *assegai* into his stomach when Dalton shot the warrior and saved the corporal's life. They all then burst through the Zulus and ran to the entrenchment.

As Cpl Scammel was putting his rifle to good use from behind the front rank of soldiers, he cried out in pain as a bullet ripped into his shoulder and he dropped to the ground. He crawled to Lt Chard and handed him his cartridges. He then asked for a drink of water and Mr Byrne quickly brought him one. But while Byrne was helping the distraught corporal he himself was shot through the head and fell dead.

James Reynolds was a thirty-four-year-old Irishman, who was taking part in his third campaign in South Africa. He had been appointed Surgeon in 1873.

Scammel was taken to the doctor, who was now using the storehouse verandah, calmly busying himself with organising and attending to his casualties and seemingly unconcerned about the violence going on all around.

To the east of the defences a number of warriors had begun to creep up to the wall of the kraal to assault it, while others were running in on the storehouse with burning torches in an effort to set fire to the roof. Sgt Windridge and Cpl Attwood were among the men defending the upper windows, and Lt Adendorff was manning a loophole in the side of the building, which gave him a clear aim at any Zulus who were creeping along the outside of the south barricade, or at those who had moved around to the back of the hospital. A warrior escaped the line of fire from the windows and reached the back wall of the store. He began to climb the wall with a tuft of blazing grass, and stretched up to make con-tact with the thatch. Lt Adendorff saw him just in time and shot him down.

Lt Chard could see that the post was now in great danger from all sides, so he gave the order that the two heaps of bags in front of the store should be converted into a high redoubt, to give them a second line of defence. This would also be the place where they could make a last stand. Mr Dunne and a few men at once began to pull sacks from the tops of the piles and stack them in two parallel lines between the heaps, leaving a hollow in the middle where the wounded could be safely put.

It was now beginning to get dark, and as the light faded they began to realise that they might be overrun by the Zulus under cover of darkness. But the smoking roof, which they had considered to be a catastrophe when it first occurred, became their saviour when it burst into flames and lit up the whole area. They would now be able to see the warriors as they attacked.

In their endeavour to keep the Zulus out, most of the defenders at the breastwork had concentrated their efforts at the north-west corner, and had left the perimeter between the cattle kraal and the place where the biscuit boxes met the breastwork dangerously undermanned. Lt Chard was giving a helping hand with the redoubt when he noticed that the Zulus were preparing to break through at that point. Lt Bromhead had just led the sixth bayonet charge to force the Zulus back from the verandah when Chard brought his attention to the serious situation behind them. Bromhead quickly called out half a dozen names and they all ran back to strengthen the section.

It was time for Lt Chard to look around the post and check the situation. Bromhead had secured the position near the kraal once again, but now the men in the hospital were hard pressed. If he decided to abandon the outer perimeter the men inside the hospital would be in great peril. But a large body of Zulus were pushing forward again and he could see that the men would not be able to hold the position much longer. He had no choice but to call all the men in the firing line back to the biscuit box entrenchment. As they retired the warriors occupied the verandah, and many more ran in on the outer perimeter and used it as cover from which to fire. The hospital building was now completely isolated.

1: ***William Allen – see p149***
2: ***Alfred Saxty – see p150***

RICHARD SCOLLINS

CHAPTER FIVE:
The Hospital Siege

'No one can guarantee success in war,
but only deserve it.'
Winston Churchill

All this time the men inside the hospital[1] were engaged in a desperate struggle, both with the Zulus who were swarming all around the building, and the fire that was beginning to blaze above them and send dense choking smoke into the rooms.

Pte Waters was in an inner front room defending a window which opened out on to the verandah. Gunners Howard and Evans were defending their north-west corner room, which also had access to the verandah, and a window from which they could fire at the Zulus who were massing at the front of the building. Behind this was the middle end room where the Zulus were fiercely assaulting the outer door, and from which there was no communication with the interior. Ptes John Williams and Joseph Williams were defending this room. They had left factories in South Wales to join the army at the same time, but they were not related. John had joined the army in a false name, his real name being Fielding[2]. There were four patients in the room.

'Struggle For Survival': A dazed and anxious patient is assisted through the escape hole into a room filled with smoke fumes from the blazing hospital roof. And the ordeal is not yet over.

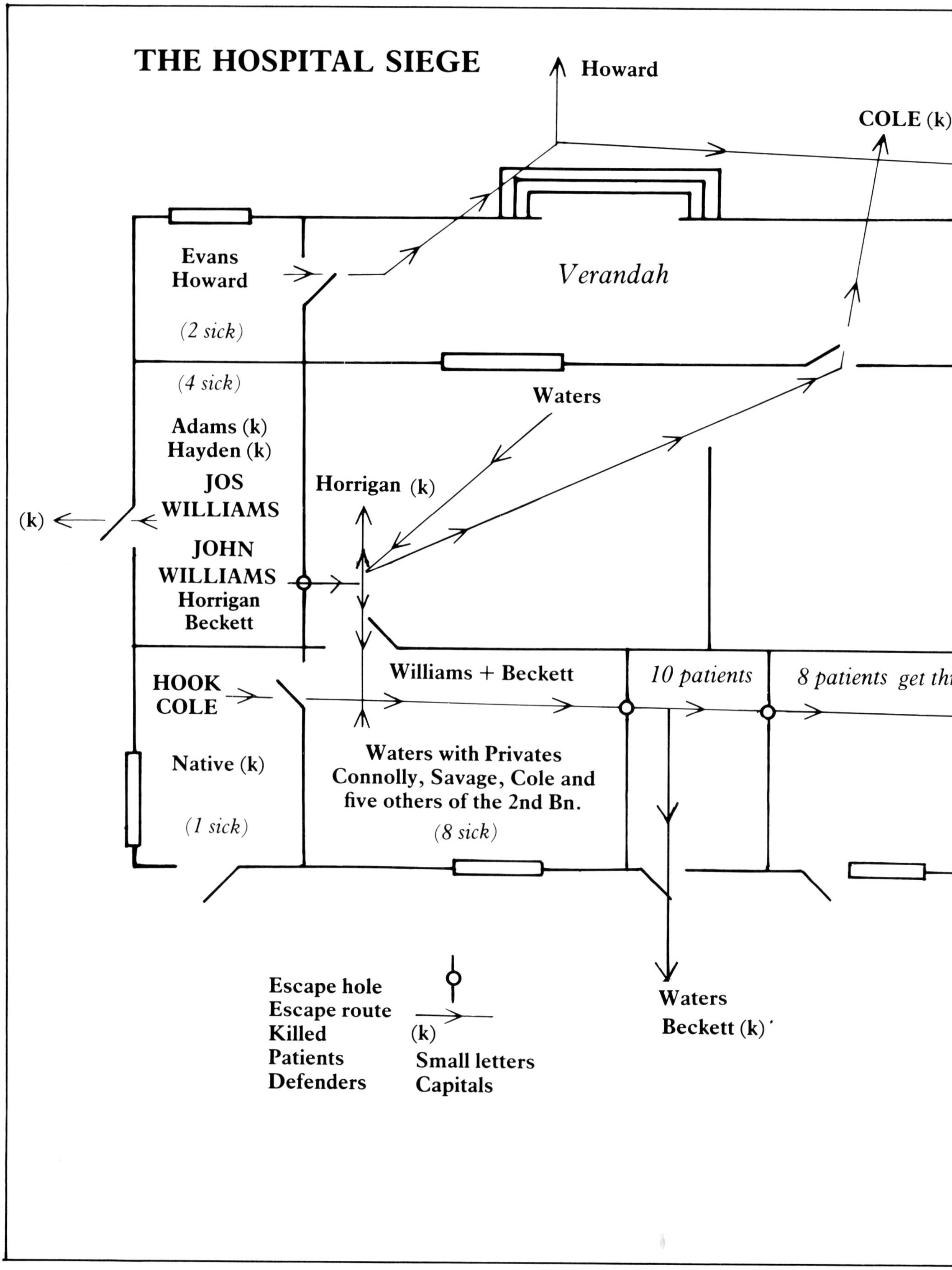
THE HOSPITAL SIEGE
Howard
COLE (k)
Evans
Howard
(2 sick)
Verandah
(4 sick)
Waters
Adams (k)
Hayden (k)
JOS
WILLIAMS
Horrigan (k)
(k)
JOHN
WILLIAMS
Horrigan
Beckett
HOOK
COLE
Williams + Beckett
10 patients
8 patients get thr
Native (k)
Waters with Privates
Connolly, Savage, Cole and
five others of the 2nd Bn.
(1 sick)
(8 sick)
Escape hole
Escape route
Killed
Patients
Defenders
(k)
Small letters
Capitals
Waters
Beckett (k)

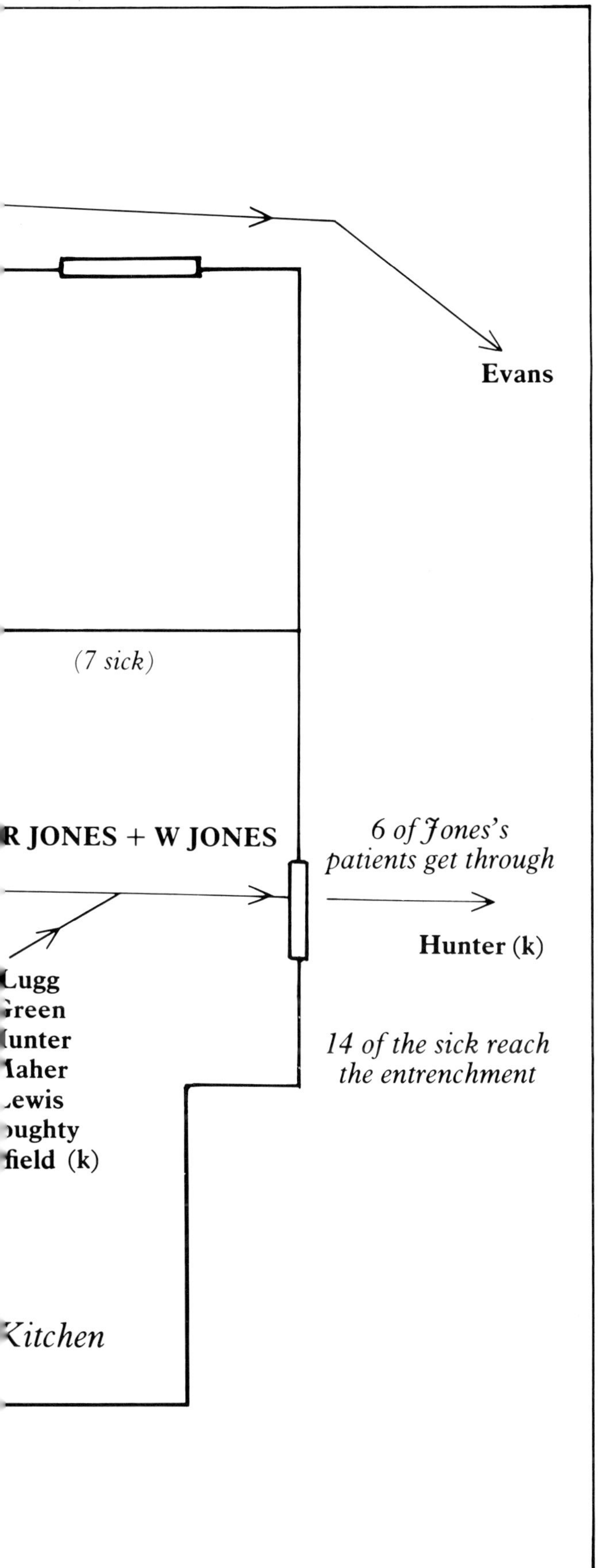

Pte Horrigan was able to offer assistance, but Pte Beckett was ill, and the other two were bedridden.

Joseph had pushed several bricks out of the wall to form a loophole the size of a small window to gain a wider line of fire. He was shooting at the warriors who were running in, throwing their weight against the door, and smashing their *assegais* at the panels trying to break it down. The patients were becoming anxious and the defenders more desperate as they realised that the door was beginning to give way. They would all be killed if they did not get out.

As soon as he had fired his last cartridge John Williams began to smash at the back partition with his bayonet, while Joseph Williams started to stab at the Zulus through the splintering door. John hacked away at the blocks to make a hole large enough to get through. By the time he had succeeded Joseph Williams had run out of bullets, and frenzied black hands were grabbing at him through the door. He fought hard to hold them back, but as John Williams and Horrigan struggled to get Pte Beckett out through the hole the Zulus forced their way in. The gallant defender was seized by the arms and legs, and Ptes Garrett Hayden and Robert Adams, both of 'D' Company were attacked in their beds. Williams was dragged outside, and all three were slaughtered in accordance with Zulu ritual. They were repeatedly stabbed, and their stomachs ripped open. The Zulus believed that this released the evil spirits from within, and prevented their own stomachs from swelling.

The three breathless men who got out of the room now eyed the area they had escaped to. They could not go left towards the verandah because Zulus were getting in that way. But through the thick smoke they could just make out the welcome form of Pte Waters, standing in a doorway to their right. Williams and Beckett got through the door but it was too late for Pte Horrigan. The warriors who had broken in behind them raced forward and set about him. They dragged him towards the verandah, threw him violently to the ground and began to stab and rip at his body. Pte Waters quickly closed the door as several other Zulus sprang for him.

Inside the room with Waters was Pte Hook and eight sick men. Pte Waters had been shot in the arm as he struggled to keep the Zulus at bay, and had retired through the inner door where he found

Hook single-handedly protecting the sick from Zulus who were trying to get in by another entrance. Hook had managed to strap up his injured arm to try to stop the bleeding.

Pte Hook and Pte Cole had defended the native, who had been wounded at Sihayo's Kraal, in a small room at the south-west corner. There was an outside door facing south and an interior door that connected with the room they were all now in. But it was above this corner room that the Zulus had first set light to the thatch, and Pte Cole had run out when the tension and fumes became too much for him. Pte Hook had then fought back the Zulus for as long as he could with the Xhosa native groaning near him and begging him for a weapon. But the struggle became hopeless. As the Zulus were breaking in he was forced to retire and escape through the interior door. The native cried out to him to help him to take off his bandages so that he could come, but there was nothing Hook could do for him. When the Zulus burst in they questioned the man, then assegaied him to death.

There were now twelve men in the room, and the

Below: *Pte Hook impales a warrior in the doorway with the point of his bayonet, as John Williams helps a patient towards the escape hole cut in the hospital wall.*

compound. Pte Savage limped anxiously across the fort and scrambled over the boxes. But Pte Robert Cole, 'F' Company, was having problems and a number of Zulus were approaching him. Pte McMahon ran to help him, and Pte Hitch added his fire-power, shooting three warriors as McMahon led Cole to safety. Cpl Allen was assisting the last few men over the boxes when a Zulu slug went right through his arm.

The whole roof of the building was now a blazing inferno, and it had become extremely hazardous for anyone who stayed inside. So the four gallant defenders who had rescued the sick decided to make their own escape. As the Zulus were scrambling into the room, William Jones, Hook and Williams climbed out. But with complete disregard for his own safety Pte Robert Jones passed his Martini-Henry out of the window, and decided to make one last attempt to save Maxfield. He groped his way back into the smoke-filled room, only to find the Zulus stabbing the helpless Sergeant as he lay on his bed. There was nothing he could do, so he quickly jumped up to the window, and heaved himself out before the Zulus noticed him. He had no sooner dropped down from the window when part of roof of the building collapsed behind him.

Pte Waters had eased the door of the cupboard open slightly, and had been shooting a few individual warriors as they left the building. But when the roof fell in Pte Beckett had run out of the cupboard, and without thinking he dashed out of the doorway, finding himself in the midst of the Zulus. A warrior thrust his *assegai* into the small of his back as he went by, but the momentum of his pace kept him going for a few more strides, and he collapsed into a ditch. The Zulus did not pursue him, but he was bleeding very badly. Eventually it became too hot and suffocating for Waters, so he covered himself with a garment that had been hanging in the cupboard, and ran out into the flickering darkness. He lay down in the long grass and rubbed dirt on his face to hide his identity.

Gunner Evans had seized the opportunity to race around the front of the hospital to the safety of the entrenchment. But when Gunner Howard ran out of the building he went the wrong way. He vaulted the breastwork, rolled off the step and crawled into bush in the shadows. The Zulus were becoming maddened by their lack of success in killing the British soldiers, and the fortification was frustrating them. They began to slay anything they could get their hands on. The three horses that had been left tied to the trees near Witt's garden wall were lying mutilated close by, and as the anxious gunner pulled loose grass over his legs to hide the stripes on his trousers, a pig was struck down near him and its squeals attracted attention. He lay uneasy among the Zulu corpses.

'Onslaught!'. While the struggle continued inside the hospital, events outside were no more certain. The defenders at the entrenchment smashed and stabbed at the Zulus, who in their frenzied state were frightening in appearance. The only retreat from here would be for a last stand in the mealie bag redoubt.

*1: **Events within the Hospital – see p151***
*2: **Joseph Williams (Fielding) – see p152***
*3: **William Jones – see p154***
*4: **Robert Jones – see p155***
*5: **John Cantwell – see p155***

CHAPTER SIX:
Behind the Entrenchment

'It is well that war is so terrible –
we shouldn't grow too fond of it.'
Robert E. Lee

Most of the fourteen patients who reached the entrenchment were taken to be attended to by Dr Reynolds, and some were able to take up places among their comrades who were valiantly defending the inner fort. As soon as Cpl Allen had his arm bandaged he helped Rev Smith to distribute ammunition. Pte Savage lay on his side and fired his rifle through a gap in the boxes, and Trooper Lugg manned a position below the eaves of the storehouse roof.

Mr Dalton was still using his rifle well. A Zulu fell almost each time he fired it, and he continually moved along the barricade encouraging the men. He brought attention to a warrior running in at the wall, and had raised himself up to full height to fire at another when he was shot through the right side of his chest. He turned pale, but he managed to keep on his feet and handed his rifle to Lt Chard. He then asked Chard to take his remaining cartridges from his pockets, and the doctor quickly

Darkness comes on as Rev Smith gives out ammunition to the defenders who are desperately trying to force the Zulus back from the entrenchment. Lt Chard thrusts forward his sword.

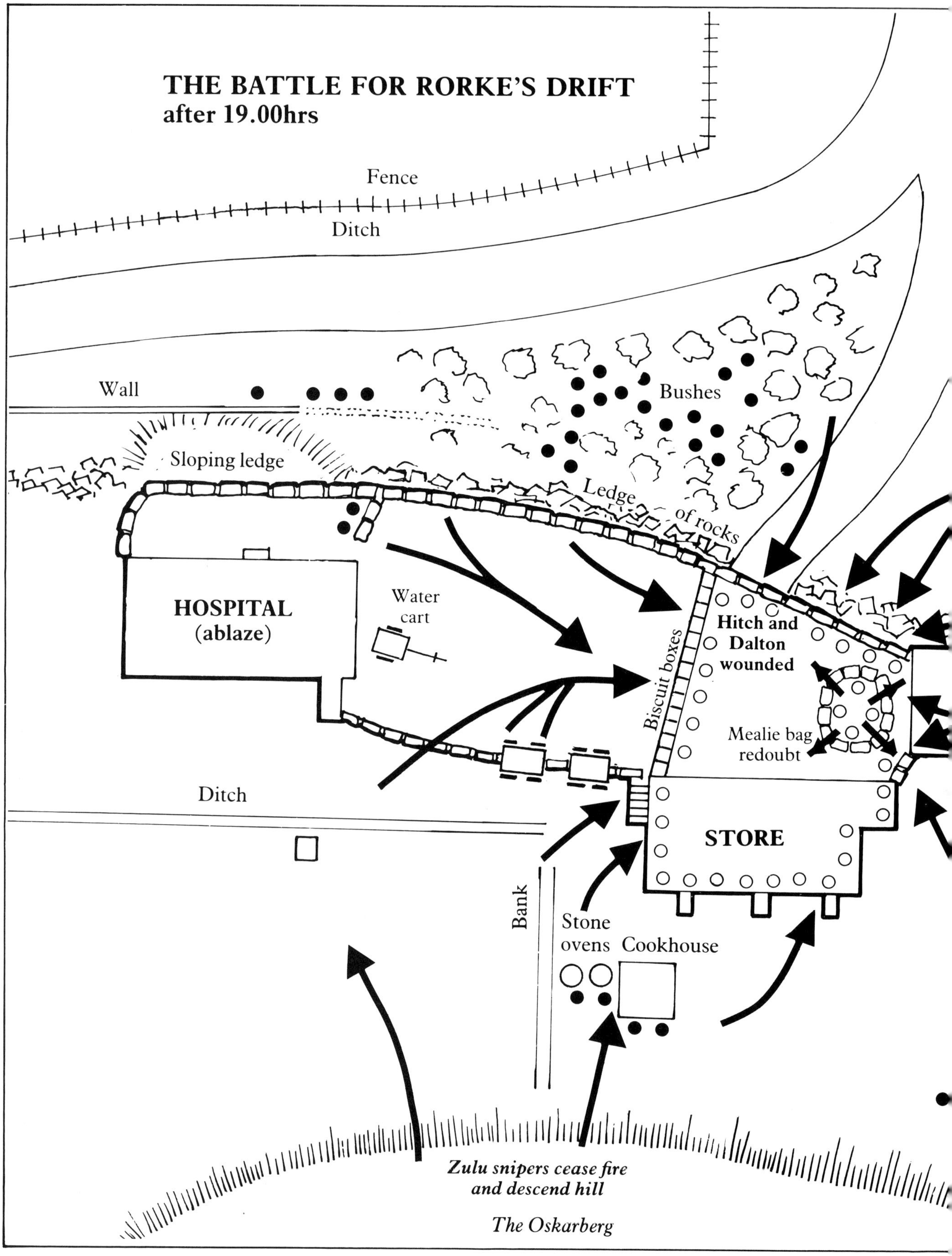
THE BATTLE FOR RORKE'S DRIFT
after 19.00hrs
Fence
Ditch
Wall
Bushes
Sloping ledge
Ledge of rocks
HOSPITAL
(ablaze)
Water
cart
Biscuit boxes
Hitch and
Dalton
wounded
Mealie bag
redoubt
Ditch
STORE
Bank
Stone
ovens
Cookhouse
Zulu snipers cease fire
and descend hill
The Oskarberg

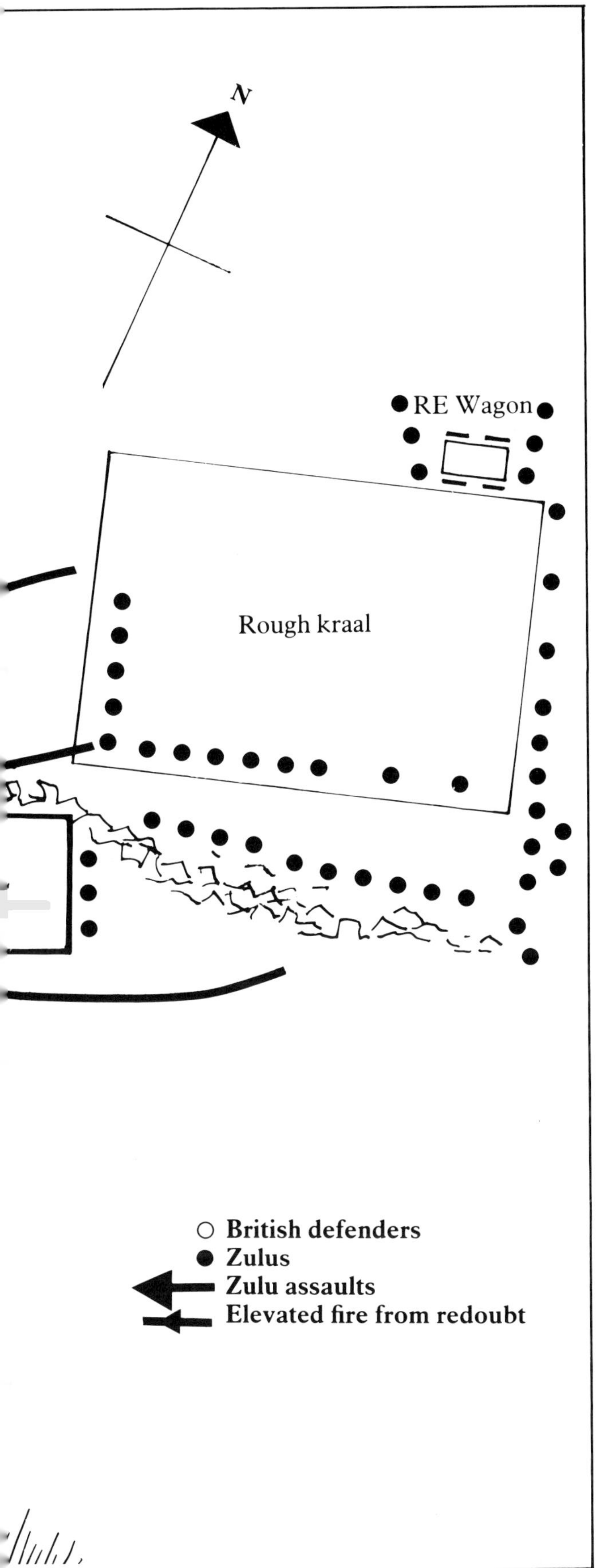

bandaged his wound. The stretcher-bearers helped him to the redoubt, and he was made comfortable as the walls were hastily raised around him.

Mr Dunne was totally exposed to enemy fire as he stood high up on the bags directing the construction. The men toiled relentlessly until the sides were about eight feet high, and they had totally exhausted themselves. Between thirty and forty men then climbed inside and the most serious casualties were also housed there.

It was now past 19.00hrs and the tremendous Zulu assault had become general all around the perimeter. The darkness, and the storehouse buildings shielded the defenders from the aim of the Zulus on the Oskarberg, so most of them came down and took cover nearer to the wall, from where they began a harassing fire. The warriors stalked out of hiding and crept up to the wall under cover of the shadows created by the light from the burning hospital, and sprang up on to the ramparts to get at the defenders. The riflemen posted at the loopholes in the western end of the store were able to keep the warriors away from the shelter of the outside of the south barricade. But to the east of the defences the men in the kraal were being pushed back.

Driver Robson was among these men. He was concentrating his fire at the Zulus who were ransacking the wagon with the engineering equipment in it. They had wrecked the camp of the Twenty-Fourth in the darkness beyond the storehouse and because the kraal was some distance from the light of the burning hospital it was not as well lit as the rest of the fort and many warriors were able to approach the walls undetected. One warrior crawled along in the darkness and grabbed Pte Michael Minehan's leg. He prodded the straw frantically with his bayonet and killed the Zulu. Eventually, however, the defenders were pushed back to the low partition, and then to the inner wall below the mealie-bag redoubt while the Zulus occupied the abandoned walls. But the walls were an awkward height and the men on the redoubt were well elevated above them. Each time a warrior presented his rifle over the wall he was easily picked off.

Lt Bromhead and the men he had brought back from the outer perimeter were still defending the much exposed area where the biscuit-boxes met the northern breastwork. A Zulu bullet hit Lance-Sgt Williams in the left side of his chest, and he fell seriously wounded. As the stretcher-bearers were taking him to the redoubt Pte John Fagan was also hit in the chest. He fell against the biscuit boxes, but managed to keep hold of his rifle and remained at his post. Ptes James Chick 'D' Company and John Scanlon 'A' Company were shot down and killed by Zulu cross fire, and Lt Chard would also have been killed if Pte Jenkins had not shouted a warning and pulled his officer's head down just as a Zulu round whizzed over it. Jenkins himself was later killed.

Lt Bromhead was keeping an eye on the ammunition, and was continually telling his men to take careful aim and not to waste rounds. As he took steady aim at a warrior near the hospital a Zulu managed to scramble over the breastwork and came up behind him with his *assegai* raised to strike. Pte Hitch saw the warrior but his rifle was not loaded and he had lost his bayonet. He could do nothing but try to bluff the warrior by putting the muzzle of his rifle on him. The ruse worked, and the startled Zulu clambered back out of the enclosure without delivering the fatal blow.

Still more Zulus sprang up and attacked the wall and so Hitch joined the men fighting to keep them back from the northern breastwork area. A Zulu attempted to climb the bags, so he blocked him and tried to force him back. As he did so he noticed another Zulu to his left who was aiming his rifle straight at him. He reeled backwards from the wall as the Zulu shot him in the right shoulder. As he fell the Zulu moved in for the kill. Lt Bromhead had been behind Hitch providing a second line of fire, and he also saw the Zulu. He levelled his revolver and shot dead the Zulu. Hitch was bleeding badly, but got to his feet, stripped to his shirt and put his injured arm into his belt. Pte George Deacon tore the lining from the sleeve of Mr Dunne's greatcoat and tied it around his shoulder to secure it. Hitch then borrowed Bromhead's revolver for a while, but began to feel ill, and eventually decided to help with the distribution of ammunition. Mr Dalton had also recovered enough to help with the ammunition.

Pte Desmond was nicked in the fleshy part of his thumb by a slug, and another found its way through a gap in the biscuit boxes and hit Cpl Lyons in the right side of his neck. He fell sprawling over the biscuit boxes and landed outside the enclosure but the defenders dragged him back in and Dr Reynolds quickly attended to him.

The Zulus who were crouching behind the outside of the perimeter wall were causing problems with their short-range fire. Cpl Schiess was concerned by the amount of damage they were doing,

Pte Jenkins aims his Martini-Henry from a kneeling position behind the breastwork at the north rampart. During the height of the Zulu assault on the entrenchment he saved Lt Chard's life. It was acts of vigilance and comradeship such as his which undoubtedly helped the defenders to survive the repeated Zulu attacks.

so he slipped over the boxes and crept along the inner side of the wall towards a group of warriors. He cautiously raised himself up before them and aimed his rifle but one of them fired first and blew his hat off. Schiess quickly jumped onto the bags, his body illuminated by the glare from the blazing fire, and bayonetted the Zulu. He then shot another Zulu close by, and as a third warrior was coming to their aid, he met him with the point of his bayonet. The gallant corporal then returned to his post.

Dabulamanzi was directing his warriors from behind Witt's garden wall. As the battle went on he was becoming more and more anxious. He had disobeyed Cetshwayo's orders not to attack fortified places, and could only justify his actions by taking back a report of unqualified victory. But he had already launched his best attacks and the soldiers were still secure in their corner of the enclosure. Even if he did eventually succeed his losses were already heavy, and mounting. Being deprived of his fellow inDuna he was finding it increasingly difficult to stir up morale in such a large *impi*, and he could see signs that they were losing heart. They were used to fighting out in the open, and not against quick-firing rifles behind frustrating forti-

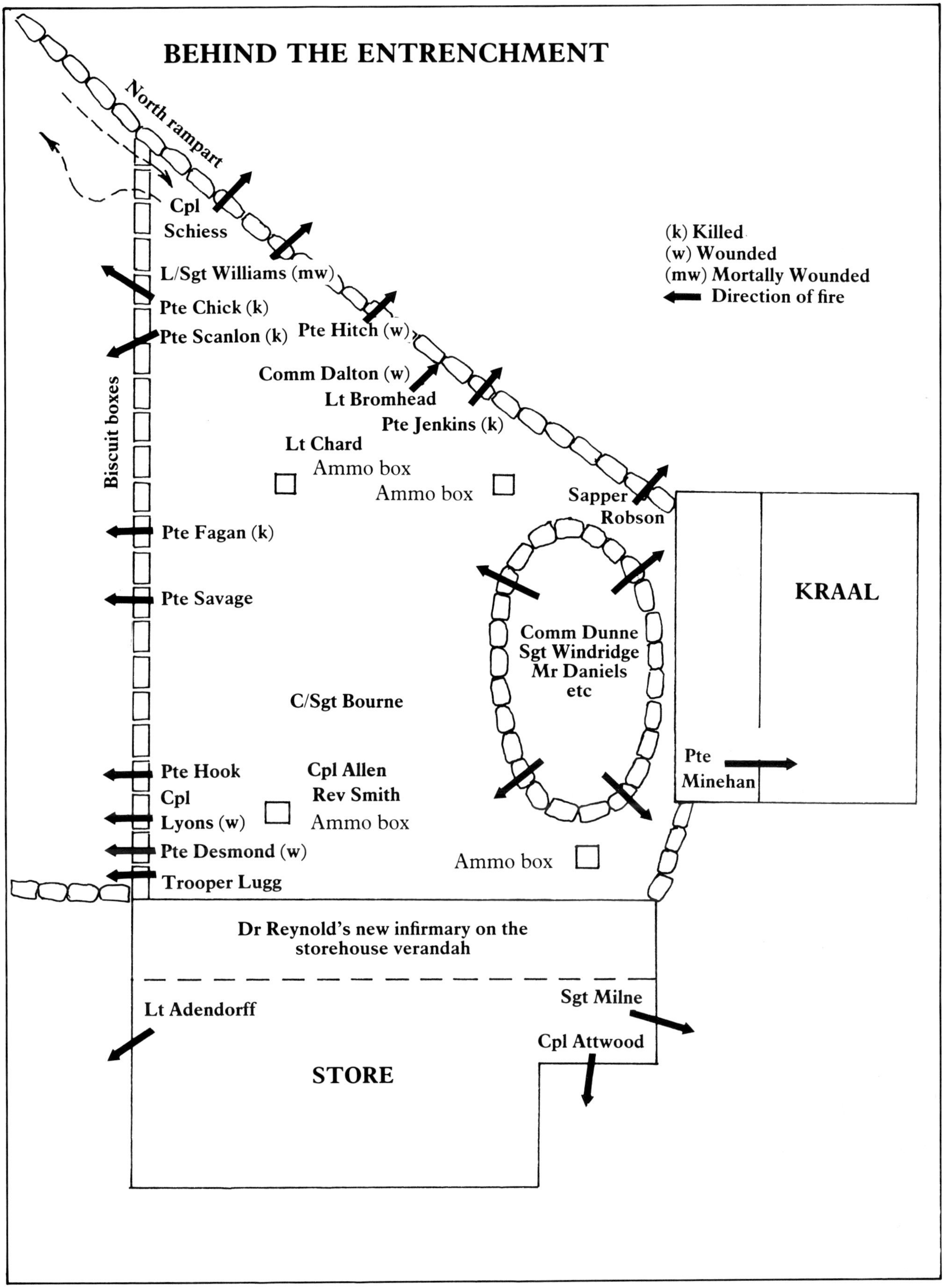
BEHIND THE ENTRENCHMENT
North rampart
Biscuit boxes
Cpl Schiess
L/Sgt Williams (mw)
Pte Chick (k)
Pte Scanlon (k)
Pte Hitch (w)
Comm Dalton (w)
Lt Bromhead
Pte Jenkins (k)
Lt Chard
Ammo box
Ammo box
Sapper Robson
(k) Killed
(w) Wounded
(mw) Mortally Wounded
Direction of fire
Pte Fagan (k)
Pte Savage
KRAAL
Comm Dunne
Sgt Windridge
Mr Daniels
etc
C/Sgt Bourne
Pte Minehan
Pte Hook
Cpl Allen
Rev Smith
Cpl Lyons (w)
Ammo box
Pte Desmond (w)
Ammo box
Trooper Lugg
Dr Reynold's new infirmary on the storehouse verandah
Lt Adendorff
Sgt Milne
Cpl Attwood
STORE

Above: *This sketch drawn by Frank Bourne to illustrate his narrative for the Listener in 1936, differs slightly from Lt Chard's, but shows the scene at the post how he remembered it.*

fications. They had not eaten properly for days, and had travelled over sixteen miles on foot before the assault.

The three defenders outside the perimeter shivered in the cold night air. Pte Waters lay nursing his wound as Zulus moved about near him. He was trodden on several times, but the darkness hid his identity and they left him alone. Pte Beckett was still curled up in the drainage ditch, with his abdomen saturated in his own blood, and he had lost consciousness. Gunner Howard had also nearly been discovered several times. He had contemplated making a dash for the enclosure, but there were too many warriors about so he lay motionless, in fear of his life.

For the defenders thirst and fatigue had now become as much an enemy as the Zulus, especially among the wounded. The water cart was near the burning hospital where it was impossible to reach without putting more men in danger. Some men tried to get at the rum casket, but Sgt Milne warned

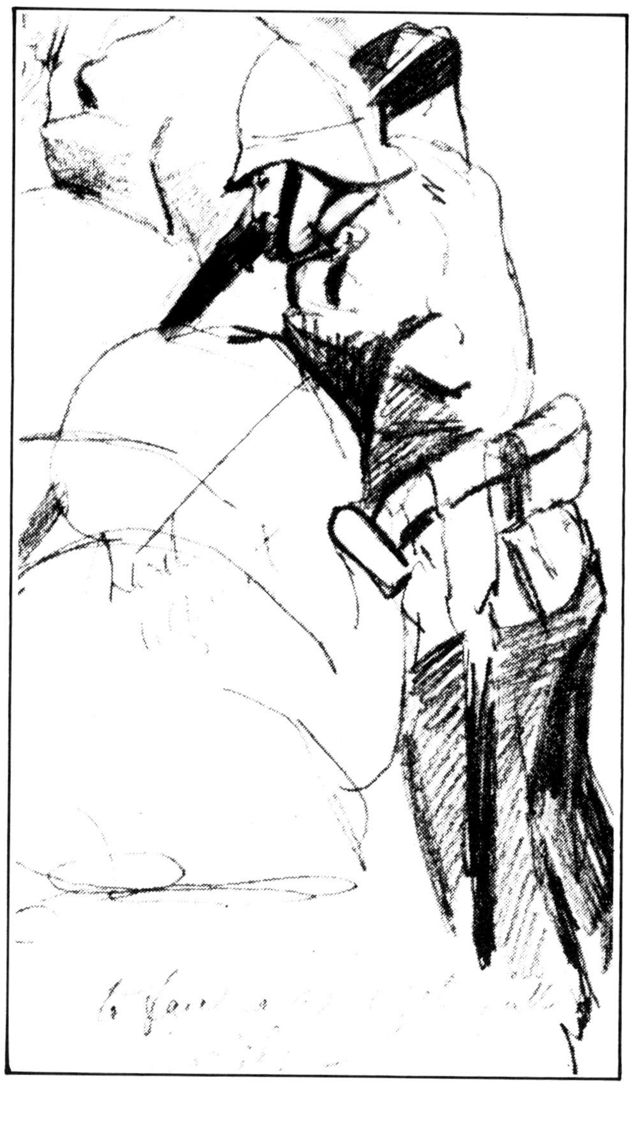

Right: *This is a preliminary sketch by Lady Butler of a soldier at Rorke's Drift in the low guard position. He appears in the finished painting farthest left of the defenders at the breastwork.*

Lieutenant Chard as he may have appeared at Rorke's Drift. He is wearing a scarlet single-breasted Engineer officer's jacket, with garter-blue facings. His buff cord riding breeches are tucked into brown leather boots. He is seen here firing a rifle, and he also carried a hand gun. He also used his sword to defend himself at close quarters.

J. NASH

Above: *Three warriors of King Mpande's army proudly display their exotic dress.*

Above: *Utimuni, Shaka's nephew, stands on parade. After taking part in a ceremonial war dance he will march past the king stooping in respect.*

Below: *The animal skin flying over this small kraal near Umlazi signifies that the inDuna is at home.*

Above: *This classic painting by C. E. Fripp, shows the survivors of the 24th Regiment rallying around the colours for a last stand at Isandhlwana. The massacre of nearly a whole infantry battalion shocked the nation and humiliated the British Government.*

Left: *'Saving The Colours', painted by Alphonse de Neuville, depicts Lieutenants Teignmouth Melville and Neville Coghill, 1st/24th Regt, during their heroic dash to try to save the Queen's colour of their battalion. They managed to reach the Buffalo River but were caught and killed by Zulus on the Natal side, at a place called Sotondose's Drift.*

Right: *The foreign service helmet worn by this sergeant has been dyed. He wears the undress serge frock with grass-green facings. The regimental badge is a brass sphinx and the '24' on the shoulder strap is of white metal. His accoutrements are part of the valise pattern equipment first used in 1871.*

R·SCOLLINS

'The Defence of Rorke's Drift, January 22nd 1879' by Lady Elizabeth Butler. This stirring painting was commissioned by Queen Victoria. Some of the 'principal heroes' were made available for the artist to study, as they were asked to re-enact their part in the action dressed in the uniforms they had worn on the day. Certain individuals have been identified in the painting. Lt Chard is in the centre, pointing, with Lt Bromhead next to him. On Chard's left, Acting Commissariat Officer Dalton flings his arm in the air as he is hit by a rifle bullet. To his left, in the white helmet, Surgeon-Major Reynolds treats a wounded man. On the exteme right, his shoulder bandaged, Pte Hitch brings up more ammunition. On the extreme left are Ptes William and Robert Jones. Behind them the Rev smith, his hand to his mouth, shouts a warning. To his left, lying on the ground, is Cpl Schiess of the Natal Native Contingent. Not all the incidents shown in the picture happened at the same time, but Lady Butler's intention was to include portraits of the eleven men who were awarded the Victoria Cross. This was the highest number ever awarded for a single action.

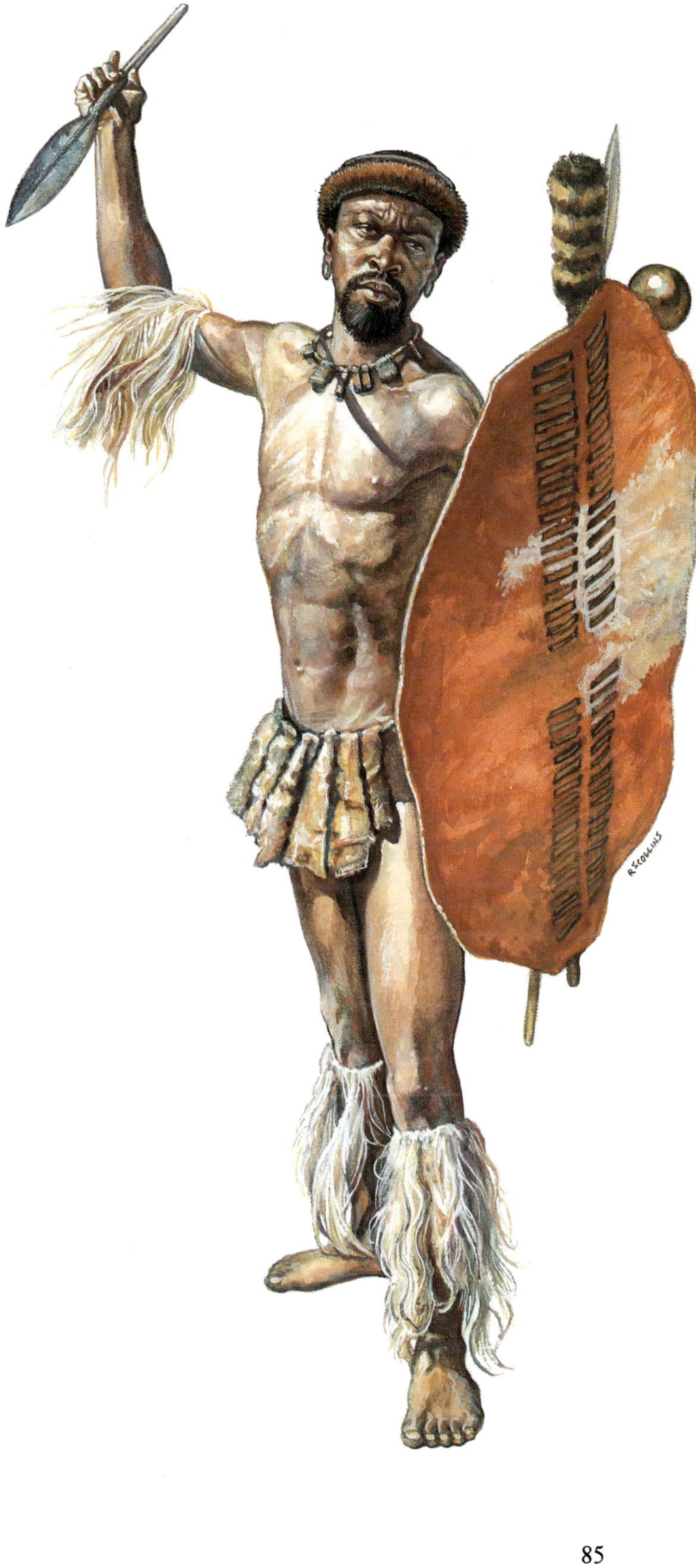

Right: *This warrior of the uDhloko regiment, following the usual practice on campaign, has jettisoned much of his ceremonial dress and retains only the otterskin headband and cowtail arm and leg decorations. Reflecting his married status he wears the headring and also a charm necklace made up of small wooden blocks and pouches of animal skin.*

Above: *The Union Jack that flew over the mission-station at Rorke's Drift during the Zulu attack.*

Left: *Lieutenant Gonville Bromhead VC, was in command of 'B' Company at Rorke's Drift. Generations of his family had served with the 24th Regiment, and he was with the South Wales Borderers when he died in 1891.*

Below: *Time and again the Zulu warriors leapt onto the barricade and tried to get at the defenders. But they were brought down by British bullets or were met with the point of a bayonet. This picture by W.H. Duggan shows the ferocity of an attack on the north perimeter.*

Above: *As Surgeon Reynolds attends to a wounded man, a soldier of the 24th Regiment is hit by a Zulu bullet and reels back from the barricade. The hospital water cart can be seen in the background close to the burning hospital.*

Right: *The British stand their ground as yet another wave of warriors assault the perimeter in their effort to wear the defenders down and break their spirit. The battle lasted for twelve hours and left dreadful memories in the minds of the survivors.*

Above: *The Dalton medals. The South Africa Medal is a replacement for the original, which was lost. Dalton's service record shows him to be entitled to the single bar 1877-78-79.*

Right: *The memorial at the grave of Colonel John Chard VC, 'The Hero Of Rorke's Drift', in the churchyard of St John the Baptist, Hatch Beauchamp near Taunton.*

Below: *The 'VC Case' in The South Wales Borderers Museum. Ten soldiers of the regiment were awarded the Victoria Cross for the Zulu campaign of 1879. Soldiers of the regiment have won twenty-three in all.*

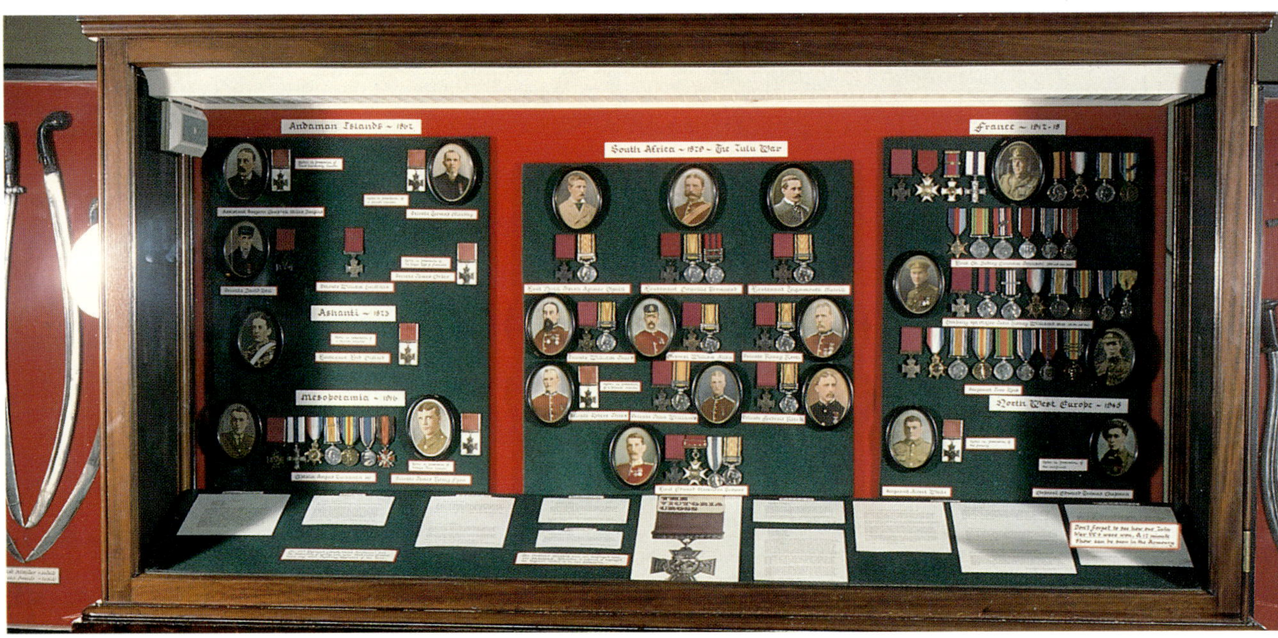

them of his orders, and he jumped on the barrel threatening to shoot any man who touched it. Eventually, the cries for water became unbearable, so a handful of men jumped over the boxes and ran to fetch some water in. Pte Fagan was supporting himself on the boxes pleading for water, and Pte Savage heard him, so he crawled along to help him. But Fagan collapsed and later died.

As ten o'clock came and went, many men were beginning to consider their situation as hopeless, and they could see no chance of escape. But they still intended to fight to the end. They had been firing continually for five hours, changing shoulders when they became bruised and sore from the recoil of their rifles, until they both hurt so much that they had to hold the weapons at arm's length to fire. The rifle barrels became so hot that their fingers and palms became scorched, and they had to use a rag to hold them. Others picked up the weapons of their dead and wounded comrades and used them alternately. They had frantically to clear the barrels with a ramrod when they fouled up and jammed, and their hands became cut and splintered as they fumbled for cartridges in the ammunition boxes. The bayonets were effective, but they were not strong, and most of those that had not snapped from the rifles had bent during the struggle. Their clothes were ripped and begrimed, and their faces were dirty and splashed with blood. Some men could no longer speak from exhaustion and the smoke that parched their burning throats.

Chard and Bromhead joined the men in the redoubt to get a better view of the situation. The hospital fire blazed on, and although it had completely destroyed the medical supplies, it still enabled the defenders to keep the Zulus in view as they approached the barricade. Chaplain Smith was praying that the warriors would go away, and the men who could no longer fight encouraged those who could. Pte Hitch was moving along the barricade giving out cartidges when he began to feel faint and thirsty. He collapsed with his back against the boxes close to Pte Deacon. Deacon saw that Hitch was losing consciousness and asked him if he would prefer to be shot when it came to the end. Hitch declined the offer before he passed out, and he was taken to the shelter of the storehouse.

Towards midnight the attacks became less frequent, but the Zulus kept the soldiers on constant alert. Dabulamanzi was still trying to stir up aggression in his tired warriors, and the ground shook as they stamped their feet and clashed their shields in the darkness. On one side of the post the commands of the Zulu leaders would call out, and a cry of 'Usuthu!' would follow. The men defending that area would then strain their already weak and sore eyes, and prick their ears to detect an attack. But then the same thing would happen at a different point around the perimeter, and another section would be alerted. They could never be sure from where the next Zulu attack would come. Dark shadowy figures would then run up to the barricade, and as they became illuminated by the glare from the fire the defenders shot most of them down as they approached. The few who reached the wall clambered up the bodies of their dead and pounced on the defenders. But the shock of sharp steel always met them and they died.

The fire began to burn itself out, and as a pale light appeared from behind the Oskarberg, some men were daring to think that they might still be alive to see the dawning of a new day. The battleground became still, but now and again some rafters or timbers would collapse in the building, and as flames and sparks rose up from the embers new targets were illuminated and a few shots were exchanged. Then all became silent again, but for the cries of the wounded and dying. Those Zulus who had been too gravely wounded were put out of their misery by their fellow warriors with a sharp *assegai* thrust under the armpit. Brave and gallant men from totally different cultures, who had been brought together in conflict, had earned a deep respect for each other.

Towards morning the soldiers became suspicious of a longer than usual silence. But at last the dull light rose from behind the hills and glimmered across the sky, and the streak of dawn moved across the shattered post. And as the defenders looked out beyond the hundreds of black corpses were scattered all around, groups of dejected and spent warriors could be seen retiring over the rise from where they had appeared twelve hours earlier. They dragged many of their wounded and dead away on their shields, but some warriors could be heard groaning among the carnage.

CHAPTER SEVEN: *The Smoke Clears*

'It seemed that out of battle I escaped . . .'
Wilfred Owen

The early light revealed a devastating scene of carnage. The defenders could hardly believe their eyes at the sight of what men are capable of doing to their fellow men under the dreadful banner of war. The burned-out hospital was still smouldering, and the charred remains of the men who had died in the building smelt awful. Around the hospital and all along the breastwork were piled hundreds of Zulus, many with horrible injuries. Their limbs were tied in knots, and broken and bent from the blasts of rifles. Some warriors had been pinned to the ground by the bayonets that had killed them. Trampled grain, pot-holed tins and used cartridge cases from the twenty-thousand rounds of ammunition that had been expended were strewn all around, and the fortifications were stained with blood.

A Zulu who had feigned death in the kraal got up and fired his rifle at the defenders as they began to move about the barricade. Then he fled towards the

As news of the epic defence of Rorke's Drift began to reach England, wildly inaccurate jingoistic sketches such as this view of the post began to appear in British newspapers during March 1879. The arrow points out the approach of the relief column.

Above: *Rorke's Drift today: The stone pillar in the foreground is a national monument erected on the site where the two wagons were incorporated in the line of defence.*

Below: *The area where the biscuit boxes met the north perimeter of mealie bags, which has been marked out by a line of stones. To the right a chapel stands on the sight of the original storehouse.*

river. His shot did no harm, and he had taken everyone so much by surprise that by the time a few shots were fired after him, it was too late and he got away.

Pte Waters had taken refuge in the cook house and was so relieved to see red coats moving about the post, that without thinking he came out and approached the wall. Several rifles were trained on him at once, but he managed to identify himself just in time. Gunner Howard had also surived his ordeal, and Chard's wagon driver came stumbling in.

Nobody believed that they had seen the last of the Zulus, and although many of the men could hardly move their aching limbs, Lt Chard kept them busy repairing the perimeter and preparing for any renewed attack. He also hoped that this would prevent them from dwelling on their uncertain situation. They put ropes through the loopholes in the blackened walls of the hospital and pulled them down. The thatch was stripped from the roof of the store and piled into the kraal. The bushes and trees were cut down as much as possible, with the dead horses being left tied to the stumps. Two men tied a piece of white material to a length of wood and got up onto the roof of the store to act as lookouts. They were to give warning of any Zulu advance by waving the flag.

Patrols were sent out, cautiously watching for any surprise attack. They collected all the Zulu rifles and ammunition they could find, and brought in hundreds of *assegais* that had been left around the defences. Many warriors were still alive, and shots rang out now and then as they tried to get away when they were discovered. As Trooper Lugg limped about among the dead, he saw a rifle on the ground, and was going to pick it up when a Zulu who had been lying close by rose up and jammed the barrel against his body. The trigger clicked, but the weapon misfired. Before the Zulu could recover, Lugg dropped on him and stabbed him with his hunting knife. Pte Hook was following the course of a dry stream as he was patrolling near the river carrying a pile of *assegais*. Suddenly, he came upon a Zulu lying still on the ground. The man was unarmed, and though Hook saw blood running from a wound in his leg he suspected a trap. As he passed him Hook watched for any others who might be about to ambush him, but the warrior on the ground suddenly sprang into action and grabbed hold of his rifle. As the Zulu tried to wrestle Hook to the ground, he dropped the pile of *assegais* he had been carrying and hit the Zulu in the chest, then

At the time of the centenary, parts of the perimeter were marked out and included these two wagons, which are identical to those of the period. The building stands on the site of the hospital.

stepped back as he loaded the rifle and shot the warrior through the head. After these incidents the men were allowed to leave the fort only in numbers.

There were twenty-seven casualties. Eleven soldiers of the 24th Regt had been killed, and a twelfth was added when Pte Beckett was found alive but mortally wounded. Dr Reynolds did all he could to save his life, but he had lost too much blood and he died later. The bodies of the dead defenders whom the Zulus had managed to get hold of had been treated horribly. The corpse of Joseph Williams was found badly mutilated, but he had sold his life dearly, for there were many Zulu bodies scattered about the area that he had defended. The bodies of Ptes Hayden and Adams had been badly burned, but it was still possible to tell that Hayden had been stabbed sixteen times, his stomach had been slit open twice, and part of his cheek had been cut off. Their corpses, along with those of Horrigan, Maxfield and the Xhosa native were removed from the ruins of the hospital and placed in the kraal. One man's head had been split open, and another man, who still had his rifle pointing over the parapet, had been hit between the eyes by a Zulu slug, which had taken the back of his head away but left his face perfect except for a little hole. Trooper Hunter had received six stab wounds, and one of the Zulus had

The remains of the hospital are still smouldering, and Zulu corpses litter the area, while the defenders wave their arms to welcome the mounted infantry as it approaches the post from the drift. This is Crealock's interpretation of the scene at Rorke's Drift when he returned on 23 January, with Lord Chelmsford and the remains of the column.

been shot and killed as he was cutting up the corpse of a dead man. His stiffened body was still leaning over his victim when he was found.

Dr Reynolds continued to attend to the wounded. He took thirty-nine pieces of bone from Hitch's shattered shoulder joint, and dressed the neck wound suffered by Cpl Lyons. The ball had passed down his body and struck his spine, where it lodged. There was little he could do for him under the circumstances, but try to nurse him back to strength. The bullet that hit Lance-Sgt Williams had passed through him but he was very ill. Pte Waters had a hole four inches deep in his shoulder. Dr Reynolds applied a temporary dressing, and intended to cut the bullet out later that day. Several other men had minor lacerations and less serious injuries.

Lts Chard and Bromhead assessed the situation. There were fewer than two boxes of ammunition left in reserve, which meant that each defender had about twenty cartridges. Some men had slumped down behind the barricade to rest their aching limbs, while others shivered with cold, and the effects of shock, after a hard-fought battle. They had no idea if or when another assault might begin, but even though the men had fought far beyond their expectations, and morale was still high, they knew that if the Zulus continued to attack they would eventually be worn down, and would lose the will to fight. When the work of repairing and securing the defences was done, they returned to their places at the perimeter, and waited in an almost unbearable state of uncertainty.

At about 07.00hrs the signalmen drew attention to the south-west, where a large body of Zulus had advanced over the rise and were waiting menacingly. And then the white flag was waved for a second time, as the lookouts brought attention to a line of men that was winding down through the Bashee Valley, coming towards the river and about an hour's march away. It was impossible to tell if they were British or Zulu. But if they were the latter, the defenders' fate was sealed. They had no real ideas what had become of the rest of the column and even had they survived they might well have assumed that Rorke's Drift had fallen, and had made their way direct to Helpmekaar.

A young kaffir then came running up to the barricade. Daniels could speak a little Bantu, so Chard asked him to interrogate the native. He was found to be friendly, so Chard sent him on to Helpmekaar with a note explaining the situation and requesting immediate reinforcement.

Eventually the defenders could see the approaching force more clearly through field glasses, and hopes were raised when they could see red tunics among them. But it was then suggested that these men could be Zulus dressed in the uniforms of the men who had fallen at Isandhlwana. The Zulus on the rise were gradually moving forward, but they also seemed to be equally unsure about the advancing force. The weary men in the fort watched anxiously, not knowing what to expect. Suddenly, there were hysterical shouts from the roof of the store, and the signallers began waving the flag frantically. A body of mounted men was approaching the river. They were British. The men were overcome with relief and some cried with joy. Wild cheers rang out and helmets were thrown into the air. On the rise, a Dabulamanzi turned his dejected warriors away, and they disappeared around the hill. Lord Chelmsford was returning with the portion of the column that he had taken out from the base camp at Isandhlwana on the previous day.

At 08.15hrs, Major Russell of the 12th Lancers brought an advance detachment of mounted troops up to the post. He was anxious to know if any of the men from the Isandhlwana base camp had managed to escape to Rorke's Drift. But Lt Chard informed him that very few survivors had passed the post on their way to Helpmekaar, and most of these had been colonial volunteers. They were stricken with grief at this reply. Lord Chelmsford and his staff arrived shortly afterwards. He was dejected and emotional, and thanked the defenders for what they had done. The main body of the column then began to arrive.

They had lost everything, including their pride, and they were weary and hungry. While the mission-station had been under attack they had spent a restless night among the death and destruction at Isandhlwana. Zulu campfires could be seen on the hills all around them, and as they looked towards Rorke's Drift, the light from the burning hospital illuminated the night sky. As they had approached the river they passed Dabulamanzi's *impi* as it was moving away from the battle at the Drift. A few stragglers at the rear of the columns had exchanged shouts, but apart from that they passed each other without incident.

The Commissariat provided them with bread, biscuits, and tins of corned beef, and there was reasonably fresh water. It was their first food for two days. Colour-Sgt Bourne then issued a welcome tot of rum. Many men moved about the post anxiously looking for their friends. Neither Sub-Lt Griffith nor Pip's master were among the survivors. Many men lost close friends, and some districts of South Wales would be devastated by the loss of several of their menfolk. The defenders had been continually on alert for eighteen hours, but they were far too unnerved and tense to sleep. As they wearily began to reflect on the events they were gradually coming to realise that they had taken part in an action that might very well be considered special. Every man was thankful that he had survived the terrible ordeal.

Lt Chard was without his tunic as he washed his powder-blackened face in a muddy puddle, along with Pte Bushe, who was covered in blood from his injury. Bushe offered to share his dirty towel with Chard, and the Lieutenant accepted thankfully. Chard then went to check his wrecked wagon. It was a mess but the Zulus had left an unbroken bottle of beer, so he and Bromhead celebrated together.

Pte Hook was sent back to his duty of making tea for the sick. However, a sergeant came up and told him that he was to drop everything and report to the officers at once. So Hook found himself standing before Lord Chelmsford in his shirt sleeves and with his braces dangling at his side, giving him his account of the action in the hospital. Capt William Penn-Symons, 24th Regt, wrote down everything that was reported.

Look-outs were posted and mounted patrols were sent out. The natives were ordered to collect stones from around the post so that a more permanent loop-holed fort could be constructed. The Zulu weapons and shields were thrown into a ditch and burned, and the kaffirs were also to dig two deep pits in front of the hospital so that the corpses could be buried. The natives disliked touching dead bodies, so it took the soldiers nearly two days to collect the 351 corpses from around the post and bury them. Recent events had turned the men bitter and some wounded Zulus were also thrown in. One pri-

The New Camp, Rorke's Drift. The confined, insanitary conditions at the mission-station affected the troops badly, and as the official lists record, many men died of disease or became seriously ill while they were stationed at Rorke's Drift. The situation was only improved when a more spacious camp was established a quarter of a mile away.

vate with a Zulu prisoner reported to the officers and he seems to have taken them literally when they told him to dispose of the captive. Lt Smith-Dorrien had escaped from Isandhlwana, and when he returned to Rorke's Drift he found two head-ringed Zulus hanging from the transport appliance that he had built. Many Zulus were found between the post and the place where the *impi* had recrossed the river, and scores of blood-stained shields were also found on the banks. Some warriors had crawled long distances from the battlefield to die in dignified solitude, and for months afterwards their stiffened corpses were found in the bush and in caves in the area. It is believed that, in all, over five-hundred Zulus had been killed.

On the 25th January Lance-Sgt Williams finally succumbed to his wounds and he was buried with the others. Seventeen of the defenders were officially recorded as killed in action. This number included the Xhosa Native and Cpl Anderson. Thirteen soldiers of the twenty-fourth were buried close together, and later a wall was built around their graveyard. A makeshift wooden cross was at first put up, but afterwards an obelisk-shaped stone monument was erected in the centre of the little cemetery. A bandsman named John Mellsop used pieces of broken bayonets to carve out the names and a picture of the fight.

For the gallant defence of Rorke's Drift eleven men were later awarded the Victoria Cross, more than for any other single action in British military history. Four men were awarded the Silver Cross for Distinguished Conduct in the Field. Chard and Bromhead received accelerated promotions to Brevet-Major, dated 23rd January 1879, and they both received the thanks of the House of Commons. Surgeon Reyonolds was promoted to Surgeon-Major dated 23rd January 1879, Sgt Milne was promoted to Colour-Sgt on his return to Canterbury, and Colour-Sgt Bourne was offered a Commission. Five other NCOs of 'B' Company were also promoted from 23rd January 1879, but they were all reduced later. Rev Smith was given a permanent commission as Chaplain to the Forces, and there were also a number of civilian presentations.

In the days that followed, as the men exchanged stories and details, they were able to piece together the events of the 22nd January. The defenders learned that when Major Spalding had arrived at Helpmekaar, he found that the officer in command there had held back the company of the 1st Bn, because he felt that he could not spare them until reinforcements had reached him. Spalding over-

Below: *The men who held Rorke's Drift. A truly historic picture of the survivors of 'B' Company, 2nd/24th Regt. Lt Bromhead is lying down on the far left of the front row.*

Left: *Many men used their civilian skills when on Active service. Here a burial team builds the monument and engraves the stone with the names of the dead. Rorke's house can be seen in the distance.*

ruled him, and ordered a detachment of troops to follow him back to the mission-station. The Major rode on in front, and about three miles from Rorke's Drift he came upon some abandoned wagons, a number of which were still loaded. He then met several fugitives fleeing towards Helpmekaar, including Ptes Grant and Johnson, whom he ordered to return to Rorke's Drift with him. About a mile further on they met Lt Henderson and Bob Hall, who brought attention to a column of smoke rising from the hills in the direction of the Drift. Although the buildings were not visible, Major

Spalding accepted their report that the post had fallen into Zulu hands. They then saw a number of natives blocking the road ahead, so Spalding decided to turn back, and take the two companies of the 1st Bn to prepare to defend Helpmekaar. It was never ascertained if these were the red-coats that the men in the garrison had thought they had seen soon after the Zulu attack started.

Lord Chelmsford questioned Major Spalding's decision, and this became a point of controversy. But then some of the actions and decisions of senior officers at Isandhlwana could also be considered folly and insurbordinate.

Below the mountain at Isandhlwana, because the base camp was only a temporary one, they did not laager the wagons. This was a difficult manoeuvre to perform, and the Natal kaffir wagon drivers did not have the skill to manage it. The ground was considered too rocky to make an effective entrenchment, but there was a steep *donga* running across the face of the camp, and the slopes of Isandhlwana hill gave adequate protection at the rear. Look-outs were posted on high ground to the north, where the Nqutu plateau would hide any Zulu advance until it was very near the camp. Vedettes were also posted in other strategic places.

Lord Chelmsford had left nearly six-hundred regular soldiers in the camp, made up of five companies of the 1st Bn and most of 'G' Company of the 2nd Bn. There were two 7-pounder field guns, and when Colonel Durnford arrived with his detachment of troops at about 10.30hrs there were 1,800 men to guard the camp.

But Colonel Durnford did not stay. Although command of the camp had devolved on him, he moved out across a plain in front of the tents with a section of his men and the rocket battery, to pursue a Zulu *impi* which had been sighted in that direction. He had sent some of his Basutos out scouting earlier, and they came upon a party of Zulus herding cattle about four miles north of the camp. They chased them over the edge of a ridge, but suddenly found themselves staring open-mouthed into a ravine. Covering the slopes and sides as far as they could see were thousands of Zulu warriors squat-

By 22 January 1879 the British had established themselves at the foot of Isandhlwana. When Col Durnford went out on a sortie, the Zulus attacked the ill-prepared camp and annihilated the weakened force left to guard it.

ting in silence. They had located the main *impi*. As they quickly withdrew to warn the camp, 20,000 Zulus swarmed after them.

The British troops had already been called to arms and had turned out to meet them. Colonel Durnford had also been attacked, and was being driven back towards the camp. So Pulleine deployed his men in extended lines across the plain to try to give him support. Durnford's force then lined the *donga* to make a stand and the heavy volleys from the ranks of infantry temporarily checked the Zulu advance. But they began to run short of ammunition. The swift Zulu onslaught had taken the Quartermasters by surprise, and they found it impossible to open the heavily fastened boxes quickly enough to replenish the ranks. As the Zulus took advantage of the lull in fire and raced forward, the native contingent broke and fled, leaving wide gaps in the British lines. The Zulus moved in.

The British soldiers found themselves cut off, and when they realised that they were being overwhelmed they turned back to back for their last stand. Colonel Durnford and his men had been pushed back to the camp area, and were also

engaged in a desperate hand-to-hand fight. Many warriors died at bayonet point before the British soldiers were finally wiped out. Not one single red-coat escaped, because none of them tried to, and they fought bravely until they died where they stood.

The uNdi Corps and the uDloko Regiment had formed part of the right horn which moved around

The Zulus swarm down from the Nqutu plateau, as a detachment of British soldiers try to extend the line in an effort to support Col Durnford's force who were falling back towards the camp.

to the west of Isandhlwana mountain to block the road back to Rorke's Drift. When the men who had managed to get out of the camp encountered them, they made across broken country towards the river, and for four miles they were closely pursued by the Zulu.

With the battle clearly lost, Lts Teignmouth Melvill and Neville Coghill of the 1st Bn tried to save their Queen's Colour. They got across the river at Sotondose's Drift (now called Fugitive's Drift), but they were exhausted and the Zulus caught and killed them. Both colours of the 2nd Bn were left in the guard tent at the camp. About 450 men got out in all. Two weeks' supplies fell into the hands of the Zulus, along with two artillery guns, hundreds of rifles and large quantities of ammunition.

No one will ever know what acts of gallantry and devotion to duty were performed by the soldiers

Lts Melvill and Coghill are attacked by Zulu warriors as they desperately try to reach the river with the colours of the 1st Battalion. A memorial on the bank of the river, at what is now called Fugitive's Drift, marks the spot where they fell.

Charles Fripp's heroic painting of the 24th Regiment's last stand at Isandhlwana, shows the British soldier gallantly standing fast against an attacking foe, which had great appeal to the Victorian public. Accounts by Zulus who had fought at Isandhlwana confirm that the red-coated soldiers died bravely at their posts. A bandboy, such as the one seen in the centre of the picture trying to bring attention to the oncoming warrior, refused an offer to leave the battlefield, while the Zulus were all around him, stabbing and gutting his comrades. He stayed behind to suffer a fate that was far from glorious.

who all perished in the camp area. But three men were rewarded for their gallantry. Pte Samuel Wassall, 80th (Staffordshire) Regiment, was awarded the Victoria Cross for saving a fellow soldier from the Buffalo river in the face of great danger and under a heavy enemy fire. At that time the award was not given to soldiers who did not survive. So Melvill and Coghill received no more than a mention in a citation memorandum. But King Edward VII changed the ruling, and in 1907 they became the first men to be awarded the Victoria Cross posthumously when relatives received the medals on their behalf.

The dead on the battlefield at Isandhlwana were treated with disgusting savagery. They were disembowelled, and their entrails scattered amongst the debris. Some men were decapitated and their heads placed in a gruesome ring. But one sight more than any other sickened the men who visited the battlefield. The Zulus had seized five band-boys, and either tied them to wagons by their feet and slit their throats, or hung them on butcher's hooks by their chins, sliced them up, then cut their privates off and put them in their mouths. Because of this incident boys were never again taken on active service by the British Army.

This is how Lt Chard's official report was introduced, when it appeared in British newspapers during the second week in March 1879.

Left: *On the 21st May 1879 Colonel Drury Lowe of the 17th Lancers took a force of cavalry to search the devastated camp below the mass of Isandhlwana. In the foreground stand the wrecked and looted wagons.*

The Zulu War

Madeira, Monday

The following has been received here from Cape Town:–

Lord Chelmsford has issued the following general order:–

The Lieutenant-General commanding Her Majesty's Forces in South Africa has much satisfaction in publishing for general information the subjoined official report of the gallant defence of Rorke's Drift Post, made on Jan. 22 and 23. The Lieutenant-General feels sure that the gallant conduct of the garrison will receive most ample recognition, and trusts the example set by a few brave men, and the success that attended their noble efforts, will be taken to heart by all under his command. The odds against them were nearly thirty to one; but taking advantage of the material which lay to hand, and hastily constructing with it such cover as was possible, this heroic little garrison was enabled to resist during the space of twelve hours the determined attacks made upon them, and, further, inflicting heavy loss on the enemy, the killed alone being more than three times their own number.

Left: *Five companies of the 2nd/24th Regt, who were still stationed at Rorke's Drift, accompanied Drury Lowe's squadrons. A lone sentry stands guard amongst the carnage where many of his regiment perished.*

CHAPTER EIGHT:
Revenge

'If you can keep your head when
All about you are losing theirs
And blaming it on you . . .'
Rudyard Kipling

The invasion of Zululand had suffered a serious reverse. The gallant defence of Rorke's Drift returned some order and morale to the troops, but the colony of Natal was thrown into panic. Every frontier town expected to be attacked at any moment and barricades went up as far south as Pietermaritzburg. On the day after the battle the people at Helpmekaar were brought to arms, when hundreds of black figures came streaming over the hills towards the outpost. But they turned out to be men of the Natal Native Contingent, which Lord Chelmsford had decided to disband. The Commander-in-Chief arrived in Pietermaritzburg on Sunday, 26th January, with re-invasion already in his mind. He sent a telegraph at once, which contained a short account of the recent events, and requested reinforcements, stressing the need for cavalry units.

In early February the British newspapers repor-

On July 4 1879 the British formed a military square near Ulundi and 20,000 Zulus moved towards it for their last great battle. A hail of bullets broke the attack, the warriors fled, and the 17th Lancers delivered the final blow.

'B' Company 2/24th Regt, Major Bromhead standing far left. They were presented with a scroll of honour by the Mayor of Durban, and seven men received the Victoria Cross, the largest number ever awarded to one regiment for a single action.

ted that the troops had crossed the frontier and all was well. Communication was slow in those days, and as the public waited for an expected report of a victory of some kind, more than a thousand white men had already died. A shock-wave was sent across the nation when news of the Isandhlwana disaster came to their breakfast tables. There was a public outcry, and both Lord Chelmsford and Prime Minister Disraeli came in for much criticism. The British public had felt that the conflict with Cetshwayo's warriors was inevitable, and had shown only passing interest in the South Africa situation. But the massacre of nearly a whole British infantry battalion by half-naked, primitively-armed natives made them take notice of the Zulu affair. The appearance of Lt Chard's official report helped to heal some wounded pride, and Disraeli focused extra attention on it as a diversion away from the dreadful disaster at Isandhlwana. But stories of outstanding bravery performed by the army were commonplace, and only an overwhelming victory would be acceptable. Both the public and the military wanted revenge and reinforcements were prepared at once. The government more than met Lord Chelmsford's requests.

Meanwhile, seven companies of the 2nd/24th Regt and the 5th Company, Royal Engineers, stayed at Rorke's Drift. They had to cram into the little fort while work progressed on a more spacious stronghold a quarter of a mile away. There was heavy rain every morning, which brought the stench of the dead corpses to the surface and attracted even more flies. Swarms of bacteria-carrying insects contaminated the food and water. The water was still khaki-coloured even after boiling. Conditions were dreadful, and sickness prevalent.

'B' Company were given the privilege of sleeping in the roof of the storehouse, with a tarpaulin thrown over the rafters for shelter. But the remainder had to sleep out in the open with only one blanket and a piece of canvas to cover them. Men on guard duty cut arm holes in sacks to wear over their tunics to keep warm, and everyone had to live in their damp and soiled clothes for a month. They were kept on constant alert, and there was increasing mis-

The front cover of The Illustrated London News *for 29 March 1879, shows an artist's impresssion of the scene at Helpmekaar when the colours of the 1st Battalion, 24th Regiment were recovered. In spite of its tattered condition the colour stayed in service until 1933.*

conduct. Surgeon-Major Reynolds and his men were kept much busier than they had been during the battle.

Eventually they received new blankets and supplies, and were subsequently transferred to the new fort. But it was too late for Pte John Williams (not the VC) who died of dysentery on 5th February in the post that he had so gallantly helped to defend. Two more men of 'B' Company had died of disease before the end of the year.

Major Chard had supervised the burial parties, which made him very vulnerable to disease. His infected injection also sapped his strength and he became seriously ill with fever. On the 17th February he was sent to Ladysmith and later the *Natal Colonist* reported that he had died. But he was nursed back to health by friends, and on the 29th April he reported for duty at Landman's Drift, where General Wood was organising a Flying-Column of over three thousand men in preparation for the re-invasion of Zululand.

Pte Hook had transferred to 'G' Company, and had been appointed servant to Major Wilsone-Black, who on the 4th February took a detachment of troops to Fugitive's Drift. They found the *assegai*-riddled bodies of Melvill and Coghill, and after they had buried them, the Rev Smith read a short service over their graves. To everyone's relief the Queen's Colour was recovered from the river and was proudly carried back to Rorke's Drift, where it was received with scenes of emotion. Both colours of the 2nd Bn were lost.

Otto Witt arrived in England on 5th March 1879, and with him, Umkwelnantaba. Witt had no sooner stepped off the *Warwick Castle* at Plymouth than he was selling his story to the press. After taking the awe-struck youth on a tour of London, he travelled about the country giving talks on his experiences in South Africa. He made an attempt to sue the crown for £600 in compensation for the damage at Rorke's Drift, but he could not produce documents to prove that the property was legally his, and his claim was unsuccessful. He returned to Sweden before the end of the year.

Dabulamanzi and his warriors were considered cowards when they returned to Ulundi. The prince tried to play down his failure to take Rorke's Drift by stressing that he had been successful in burning the hospital. The criticism was unjustified for they had fought bravely, and it had been their bad tactics not lack of courage that lost them the battle. Dabul-

amanzi had followed Cetshawayo's instruction to try to conserve energy whilst on the move and advanced at a leisurely pace, giving the garrison time to prepare. His method of assault was to attack the ramparts in sections, instead of launching his whole force in one over-whelming rush.

Dabulamanzi was eager to regain some honour, and took the uDloko south to join the regiments that were blockading Colonel Pearson's column near Eshowe. The uNdi Corps joined the regiments under Tshingwayo and Usibebu, who were moving towards Khambula Hill to attack Wood's column. It was estimated that nearly two-thousand warriors had been killed at Isandhlwana–Rorke's Drift, and on the same day four hundred more had died when an *impi* was repulsed by Pearson's Column as it crossed the Nyezane river on its way to Eshowe. The British however had also suffered a setback on the 12th March, when a company of the 80th (Staffordshire) Regt was almost wiped out on the banks of the Intombi river to the north. But the decisive battle of the 1st invasion of Zululand in 1879 was at Khambula.

On the 28th March a British force under Lt-Col Sir Redvers Buller moved forward from the Khambula camp to storm an enemy stronghold on the summit of Hlobane Mountain. While the skirmish was in progress, the main *impi* moving towards Khambula became aware of the fighting and detached a regiment to assist. The British were forced to retreat, and the conduct of Buller and four other men as they withdrew down the hill towards the base camp earned them the Victoria Cross. On the following day 25,000 warriors attacked Wood's laagered wagons on Khambula Hill. A murderous fire from the British weapons left 2,000 Zulus dead on the battlefield, and knocked the heart out of them. They streamed back to their domestic kraals, many having no more stomach to fight. Another severe blow to their morale followed on the 2nd April. A large Zulu *impi* under Dabulamanzi was defeated at Gingindhlovu as it tried to prevent Lord Chelmsford's force from reaching the mission-station near Eshowe to relieve Colonel Pearson. A

A large Zulu impi *surprised a detachment of the 80th Regiment on the banks of the Intombi River. Had it not been for Col-Sgt Anthony Booth, who rallied a few men and covered the retreat of fifty others, not one man would have escaped. Col-Sgt Booth was awarded the Victoria Cross.*

1
2
3
8

Left: *While reinforcements arrive from England, General Lord Chelmsford and his staff search the hills with field-glasses in preparation for the re-invasion.*

thousand more Zulu warriors died.

When reinforcements arrived from England, Lord Chelmsford formed a 2nd Division of 5,000 men, and on the 1st June he re-invaded Zululand. But on that day another tragedy occurred. The exiled Prince Louis Napoleon of France, who had been allowed to go to South Africa as a volunteer, was out with a patrol when it was attacked by a Zulu scouting party, and he was killed. The senior officer on the patrol was severely criticised for his conduct, and the incident certainly caused more anxiety in England than the Isandhlwana affair had done.

The Flying Column met the 2nd Division on the 17th June, and the combined force was in sight of Ulundi by the end of the month. With defeat staring him in the face Cetshwayo tried to negotiate a cease-fire. He sent representatives with peace offerings, but all his efforts were ignored. A decisive battle in the open would have to be fought. On the 4th July, Major Chard, Surgeon-Major Reynolds, Commissary Dunne, and Rev Smith were part of the huge square of British troops as it moved towards Ulundi. All the main Zulu regiments, including the three that had fought at Rorke's Drift, attacked. The total

Below: *A long column of British infantry and Colonial mounted troops move through hostile country towards the Zulu capital. The Flying Column met the 2nd Division on 17 June, and the combined force was ready for the final breaking of the Zulus.*

Above: *As Ulundi burned Cetshwayo fled, and it took a carefully planned military operation to track him down. He was escorted back to Wolseley's camp by The King's Dragoon Guards and the 3/60th Rifles.*

Below: *After capturing Cetshwayo the British were uncertain what to do with him. He was exiled at Cape Town for over two years, and then he found himself on board HMS* Natal *en-route for England.*

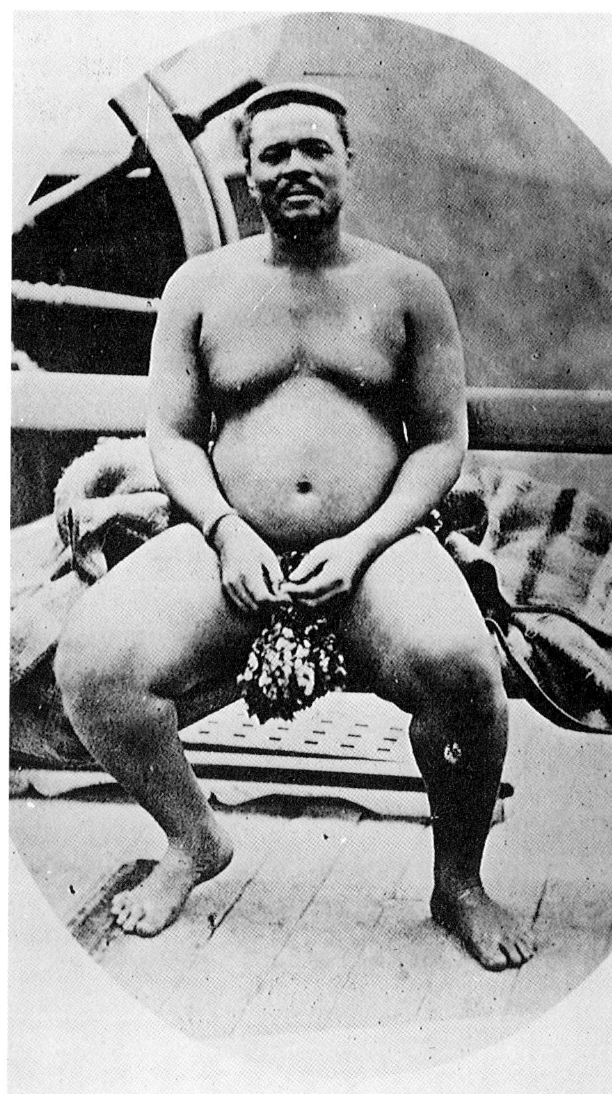

Zulu strength was about twenty-thousand warriors. The Zulus were shot down in their hundreds before they could get anywhere near the British lines, and they were finally routed and hunted down by imperial lancers. The most powerful native military machine that the African Continent had ever seen was no more.

The war was brought to a close when Cetshwayo ka Mpande was captured on the 28th August, and made a prisoner of Sir Garnet Wolseley who had replaced Lord Chelmsford. After being kept a prisoner in Cape Town castle, he was taken to London in 1882 where the man once known as an 'ignorant and bloodthirsty despot', and whose warriors had killed nearly two and a half thousand imperial and colonial troops was admired by the British public.

He was restored as king of the Zulus in 1883, but Zululand had been divided into thirteen small kingdoms and he had little overall authority. He was attacked by his old rival Usibebu and had to seek asylum on British territory. On the 8th February 1884 he was found dead in a kraal near Eshowe, and it is believed that he was poisoned. His son Dinuzulu succeeded him and Zululand, torn by civil war and with a more uncertain and fragile future than it had ever known, was annexed to the British crown three years later.

Back in southern Africa, the mayor of Durban presented each survivor of 'B' Company with a scroll of honour – 'Out of gratitude for their courage, loyalty and duty, in the face of the darkest cloud of invasion that had ever lowered over the wild frontier of British Dominion in South Africa.' The Mayor of London set up 'The Mansion House Fund' to give financial help to the widows and children of the men who had died at Isandhlwana and Rorke's Drift. Queen Victoria contributed £100, and after three months the sum had reached £6,600. Government compensation amounted to a grey shirt and a pair of trousers for each man, and they were allowed to retain their rifles. Lady Butler, who was well known for her military paintings, was commissioned by the Queen to paint a scene of the action, and many of the defenders were invited to

On his arrival in London, Cetshwayo was taken on tours of the capital in smart suits, and the British public were enthralled by him. He was invited to an audience with Queen Victoria, who presented him with a silver goblet.

CETEWAYO'S COMING!

What 'll they do with him? "No Reasonable Offer refused."

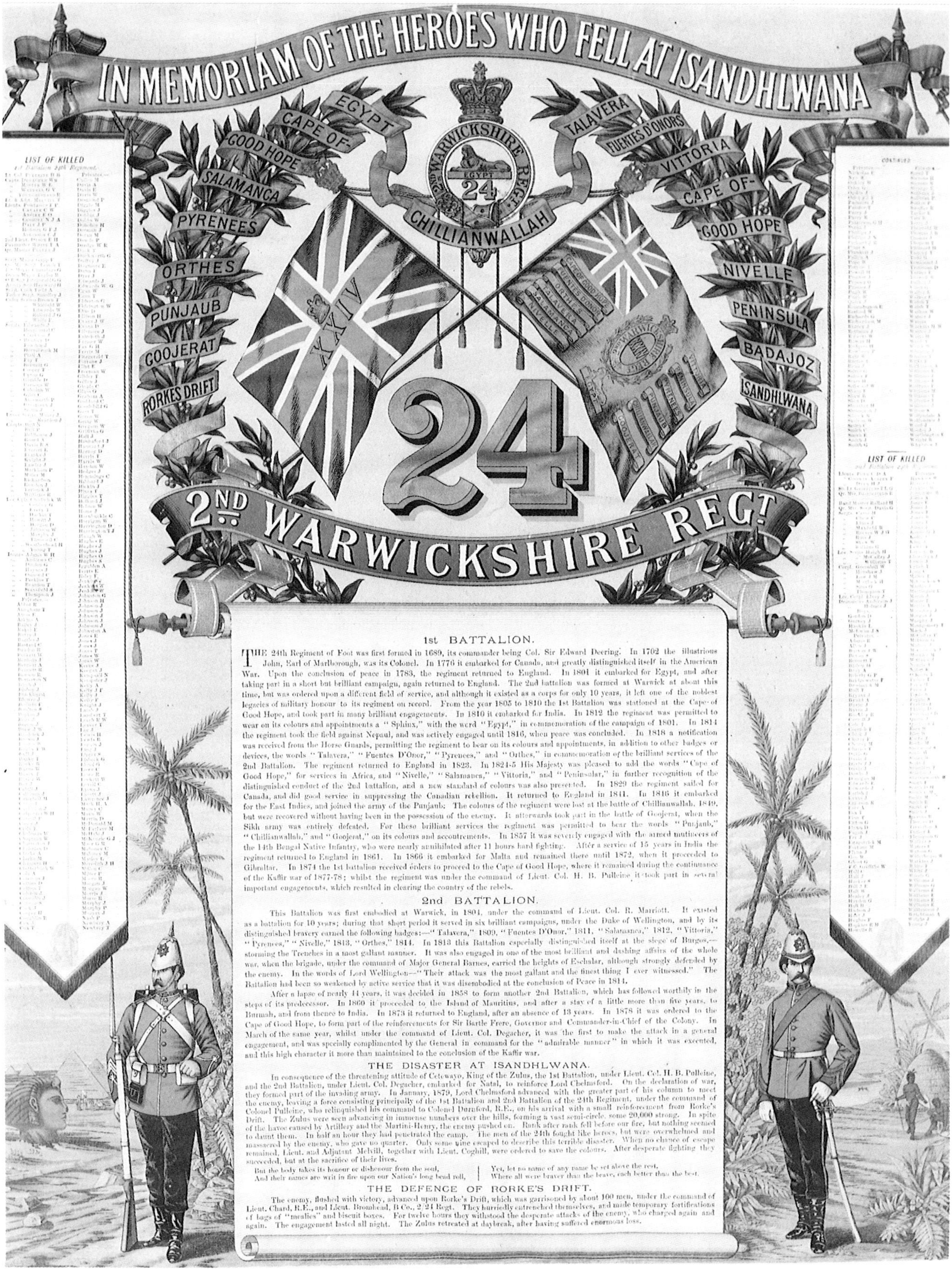
IN MEMORIAM OF THE HEROES WHO FELL AT ISANDHLWANA
EGYPT
CAPE OF GOOD HOPE
SALAMANCA
PYRENEES
ORTHES
PUNJAUB
GOOJERAT
RORKES DRIFT
TALAVERA
FUENTES D'ONORS
VITTORIA
CAPE OF GOOD HOPE
NIVELLE
PENINSULA
BADAJOZ
ISANDHLWANA
2ND WARWICKSHIRE REGT
24
CHILLIANWALLAH
XXIV
LIST OF KILLED
24
2ND WARWICKSHIRE REGT
1st BATTALION.
THE 24th Regiment of Foot was first formed in 1689, its commander being Col. Sir Edward Deering. In 1702 the illustrious John, Earl of Marlborough, was its Colonel. In 1776 it embarked for Canada, and greatly distinguished itself in the American War. Upon the conclusion of peace in 1783, the regiment returned to England. In 1801 it embarked for Egypt, and after taking part in a short but brilliant campaign, again returned to England. The 2nd battalion was formed at Warwick at about this time, but was ordered upon a different field of service, and although it existed as a corps for only 10 years, it left one of the noblest legacies of military honour to its regiment on record. From the year 1805 to 1810 the 1st Battalion was stationed at the Cape of Good Hope, and took part in many brilliant engagements. In 1810 it embarked for India. In 1812 the regiment was permitted to wear on its colours and appointments a "Sphinx," with the word "Egypt," in commemoration of the campaign of 1801. In 1814 the regiment took the field against Nepaul, and was actively engaged until 1816, when peace was concluded. In 1818 a notification was received from the Horse Guards, permitting the regiment to bear on its colours and appointments, in addition to other badges or devices, the words "Talavera," "Fuentes D'Onor," "Pyrenees," and "Orthes," in commemoration of the brilliant services of the 2nd Battalion. The regiment returned to England in 1823. In 1824-5 His Majesty was pleased to add the words "Cape of Good Hope," for services in Africa, and "Nivelle," "Salamanca," "Vittoria," and "Peninsalar," in further recognition of the distinguished conduct of the 2nd battalion, and a new standard of colours was also presented. In 1829 the regiment sailed for Canada, and did good service in suppressing the Canadian rebellion. It returned to England in 1841. In 1846 it embarked for the East Indies, and joined the army of the Punjaub: The colours of the regiment were lost at the battle of Chillianwallah, 1849, but were recovered without having been in the possession of the enemy. It afterwards took part in the battle of Goojerat, when the Sikh army was entirely defeated. For these brilliant services the regiment was permitted to bear the words "Punjaub," "Chillianwallah," and "Goojerat," on its colours and accoutrements. In 1857 it was severely engaged with the armed mutineers of the 14th Bengal Native Infantry, who were nearly annihilated after 11 hours hard fighting. After a service of 15 years in India the regiment returned to England in 1861. In 1866 it embarked for Malta and remained there until 1872, when it proceeded to Gibraltar. In 1874 the 1st battalion received orders to proceed to the Cape of Good Hope, where it remained during the continuance of the Kaffir war of 1877-78; whilst the regiment was under the command of Lieut. Col. H. B. Pulleine, it took part in several important engagements, which resulted in clearing the country of the rebels.
2nd BATTALION.
This Battalion was first embodied at Warwick, in 1804, under the command of Lieut. Col. R. Marriott. It existed as a battalion for 10 years; during that short period it served in six brilliant campaigns, under the Duke of Wellington, and by its distinguished bravery earned the following badges:—"Talavera," 1809, "Fuentes D'Onor," 1811, "Salamanca," 1812, "Vittoria," "Pyrenees," "Nivelle," 1813, "Orthes," 1814. In 1813 this Battalion especially distinguished itself at the siege of Burgos,—storming the Trenches in a most gallant manner. It was also engaged in one of the most brilliant and dashing affairs of the whole war, when the brigade, under the command of Major General Barnes, carried the heights of Eschalar, although strongly defended by the enemy. In the words of Lord Wellington—"Their attack was the most gallant and the finest thing I ever witnessed." The Battalion had been so weakened by active service that it was disembodied at the conclusion of Peace in 1814.
After a lapse of nearly 44 years, it was decided in 1858 to form another 2nd Battalion, which has followed worthily in the steps of its predecessor. In 1860 it proceeded to the Island of Mauritius, and after a stay of a little more than five years, to Burmah, and from thence to India. In 1873 it returned to England, after an absence of 13 years. In 1878 it was ordered to the Cape of Good Hope, to form part of the reinforcements for Sir Bartle Frere, Governor and Commander-in-Chief of the Colony. In March of the same year, whilst under the command of Lieut. Col. Degacher, it was the first to make the attack in a general engagement, and was specially complimented by the General in command for the "admirable manner" in which it was executed, and this high character it more than maintained to the conclusion of the Kaffir war.
THE DISASTER AT ISANDHLWANA.
In consequence of the threatening attitude of Cetewayo, King of the Zulus, the 1st Battalion, under Lieut. Col. H. B. Pulleine, and the 2nd Battalion, under Lieut. Col. Degacher, embarked for Natal, to reinforce Lord Chelmsford. On the declaration of war, they formed part of the invading army. In January, 1879, Lord Chelmsford advanced with the greater part of his column to meet the enemy, leaving a force consisting principally of the 1st Battalion and 2nd Battalion of the 24th Regiment, under the command of Colonel Pulleine, who relinquished his command to Colonel Durnford, R.E., on his arrival with a small reinforcement from Rorke's Drift. The Zulus were seen advancing in immense numbers over the hills, forming a vast semi-circle, some 20,000 strong. In spite of the havoc caused by Artillery and the Martini-Henry, the enemy pushed on. Rank after rank fell before our fire, but nothing seemed to daunt them. In half an hour they had penetrated the camp. The men of the 24th fought like heroes, but were overwhelmed and massacred by the enemy, who gave no quarter. Only some uine escaped to describe this terrible disaster. When no chance of escape remained, Lieut. and Adjutant Melvill, together with Lieut. Coghill, were ordered to save the colours. After desperate fighting they succeeded, but at the sacrifice of their lives.
But the body takes its honour or dishonour from the soul,
And their names are writ in fire upon our Nation's long bead roll,
Yet, let no name of any name be set above the rest,
Where all were braver than the brave, each better than the best.
THE DEFENCE OF RORKE'S DRIFT.
The enemy, flushed with victory, advanced upon Rorke's Drift, which was garrisoned by about 100 men, under the command of Lieut. Chard, R.E., and Lieut. Bromhead, B Co., 2/24 Regt. They hurriedly entrenched themselves, and made temporary fortifications of bags of "mealies" and biscuit boxes. For twelve hours they withstood the desperate attacks of the enemy, who charged again and again. The engagement lasted all night. The Zulus retreated at daybreak, after having suffered enormous loss.

Left: *A commemorative scroll bearing the long list of names of soldiers from the 1st and 2nd Battalions, 24th (2nd Warwickshire) Regiment, who lost their lives on the field of honour at Isandhlwana.*

pose for it.

On the 2nd October *The Eagle* docked at Spithead and the 1st Bn, 24th Regt, brought their colour home. Surgeon-Major Reynolds and Gunner Arthur Howard were also aboard, as was Major Chard, who was given a hero's welcome. A message from the Queen was awaiting him, inviting him to Balmoral. While he was there he gave her a verbal account of the defence, and she asked him to prepare for her an extended written version of his original report. The Queen liked his modest manner, and it was the first of many visits. Major Bromhead was also invited but he missed the engagement.

While the 1st Bn was stationed at Gosport in 1880, Queen Victoria requested to see the colour that had been recovered from the Buffalo river. It was taken to Osborne House on the Isle of Wight, where she placed a silver wreath of immortelles about the crown, in memory of the two men who tried to save it, and of the noble defence of Rorke's Drift. Both the colour and the wreath were laid up in the Regimental Chapel at Brecon Cathedral in 1933, where they are still on display.

When Queen Victoria inspected the colour of the 1st Battalion she placed a small wreath of silver immortelles about the crown. The wreath is now kept in a case at Brecon Cathedral.

The last nine survivors of the Rorke's Drift garrison sent a wreath to the funeral of John Fielding in 1932. Their names were: Thomas Buckley, George Deacon, Caleb Woods, John Jobbins (died 1934), Alfred Saxty (died 1936), Henry Martin (died 1937), William Cooper and George Orchard (both died after 1937) and Frank Bourne. A tenth name – Peter Caine – also appeared on the wreath, but he was at the general depot from October 1878 until April 1879, and therefore could not have been at the defence. At least four men of the garrison are known to have suffered mental illness, and many struggled with great hardship in later life.

In 1965 an American, Cy Endfield, directed the film 'Zulu', which did much to bring the defence of Rorke's Drift to the attention of the general public. William Jones's daughter, Elizabeth, who was in her eighties, travelled around cinemas in Manchester and Yorkshire to open the film. Donald Morris – another American – published 'The Washing of the Spears', which many Zulu War enthusiasts consider the most notable book on the subject. A steady flow of books and pamphlets concerning the war came out at the time of the centenary.

On Sunday, 21st January 1979, to celebrate the centenary of the battle, several corps of the Royal Engineers assembled at the grave of John Chard, with some of his family descendants. The Chief Royal Engineer laid a wreath on behalf of the Corps, and after the ceremony Chard's great-nephew, presented the Corps with a marble bust of Chard and the sword that he had carried during the defence. The curator of Taunton Museum had prepared a display of items connected with Rorke's Drift, and among the relics was a sword of honour that had been presented to Chard by the people of Plymouth. On the same day The Royal Corps of Transport at Aldershot (into which part of the Army Service Corps has amalgamated) arranged a wreath-laying ceremony at the grave of James Dalton in South Africa.

The 24th Regt became The South Wales Borderers in 1881. It amalgamated with The Welch Regt (41st Foot) in 1969, to become The Royal Regt of Wales 24th/41st Foot. They organised a concert and commemorative service at Brecon in January 1979, and sixty descendants of the Victoria Cross winners attended. Ann Jones (Miss United Kingdom), whose great-grandfather Evan Jones had been one of the defenders, took part in the celebra-

While the defence of Rorke's Drift was taking place the soldiers in the garrison at Helpmekaar manned the ramparts confused and restless. They saw themselves as the only obstacle to a Zulu invasion of Natal.

tions with the 1st Bn which was serving in Armagh. A wreath was layed on the memorials at Isandhlwana and Rorke's Drift on behalf of the Regiment, at about the same time as the commemorative service was taking place in Brecon. And a pilgrimage to South Africa was also arranged. On the 24th May 1979 the Colonel of the Regiment personally laid wreaths on both memorials.

There is a Zulu War room at the Regimental Museum in Brecon, and among the exhibits is a Bible that Harry Hook had picked up on the battlefield at Isandhlwana, and the Zulu slug that wounded Cpl Lyons. After it was extracted he had it mounted on a chain, and it was presented to the museum after his death on the 1st May 1903. There is a display case devoted to Rorke's Drift at The Royal Corps of Transport Museum at Aldershot, and there are items of interest at The National Army Museum and The Imperial War Museum in London.

The defence of Rorke's Drift had no significant effect on the outcome of the war. Some aspects of the Anglo-Zulu War are shrouded in controversy to this day, and the political and personal motives of prominent individuals connected with the conflict are questionable. But no such issues surround the ordinary men who took part in the events at Rorke's Drift. The Zulu warriors were there to gain military honour by repulsing an invader. They followed the fighting traditions of their forefathers, and beat a drum of resistance that is still being heard in southern Africa today. And the British soldiers – well, 'Theirs not to reason why': They were guardians of the empire – a job for which they received a shilling a day in wages. On the 22nd January 1879, while men in Britain were farming the land, or working factory machinery to earn their living – these men fought the Zulu!

CWT NET

CHAPTER NINE:
Notes and Tributes

'Great Occasions do not make heroes or cowards; they simply unveil them to the eyes of men.'
Bishop Westcott

When I first began this work my intention was to get as close to the facts as I possibly could, and the notes in this chapter are intended simply to express my own opinions and explain my conclusions of what happened at Rorke's Drift, not to criticise previous writers on the subject, although it has been necessary to quote some works in order to show why I needed to explain some of my points in the first place.

I always find it helpful to discover which aspects of a subject interests people the most, so while researching the book I occasionally brought up the subject of the Zulu War in conversations, of course highlighting the events at Rorke's Drift. On more than one occasion I was asked what happened to the men when they returned to civilian life. I had a basic knowledge of the lives of the Victoria Cross winners, but I had to often admit that I didn't know a great amount about any of them.

I was aware that William Jones had lived in desti-

Frank Bourne, Alfred Saxty, William Cooper, John Jobbins and Caleb Woods were the original survivors who took part in this re-enactment of the defence of Rorke's Drift for Military Tattoo held at Gateshead in July 1934.

tution for most of his life outside the army, and it had added a kind of personal touch when I had learned that he was buried in the cemetery where many of my own paternal ancestors are laid to rest. So I decided that a chapter of quite detailed biographies about the men who played the most prominent part in the action would add extra interest to the reader, especially if like myself, the soldier had a connection with their own region. The story of Pte Jones's struggle had greatly saddened me, and the tragic circumstances of the death of Pte Robert Jones, who was the second man I chose to research, had me considering whether or not I should drop the biographies idea. But I continued, eventually with much enthusiasm, and the result, I hope, will help to increase our knowledge of Britain's recognised heroes.

In a Britain where people are no longer used to hearing the call to arms, and are less willing to accept discipline than they were in Victorian times, it was proved by the operations in the South Atlantic in 1982 that the modern British soldier is still capable of going out to fight a war with the same comradeship and determination as his predecessor did over a hundred years before. The men I have chosen to record represent my tribute to all those who fought at Rorke's Drift, at the same time remembering the Zulu warriors who fought equally well, but whose names have long been forgotten.

GEORGE SMITH was born at Docking, Norfolk, on 8th January 1845. He was at college in Canterbury before going to South Africa as a Lay Missionary in 1870. He was ordained Deacon in 1871, and Priest in 1872. He was appointed to the Estcourt and Weston Missions in Natal, where he earned the reputation of a hard-working man.

For his part in the defence of Rorke's Drift his behaviour won him the praise of several men when they mentioned him in their reports about the action. He was then commissioned as Chaplain To The Forces on 1st January 1880, and he received the Zulu War medal with clasp.

After a period at home, he was in north-east Africa from 1882 until 1887. He was present at the battle of Tel-el-Kebir, Egypt, under Lord Wolseley, on 13th September 1882, for which he received the Queen's Medal for Egypt and the Khedives Bronze Star. He was present at the battle against the Dervishes at El Teb, Sudan, in 1884, and at Ginnis during the Nile Expedition, for which he was awarded a clasp. His great bushy beard earned him the nickname 'Daddy' Smith.

The Rev George 'Daddy' Smith. Following the defence of Rorke's Drift he was appointed Chaplain to the Forces and went on to serve in Egypt and the Sudan.

He was Chaplain at various stations in Britain and abroad between 1887 and his retirement in 1905. This included a spell at Fulwood Barracks near Preston from 1899 until 1903, and it was here that he eventually settled. He took a room at Sumner's Hotel, Fulwood, where he lived a quiet batchelor's life both as Chaplain, and in retirement.

He became ill with bronchial trouble, and after being confined to his room for six months, he died some time during the night of 26th/27th November 1918. His funeral was a small military parade, and among the floral tributes was one from the officers of the 24th Regt, 'In Memory Of Rorke's Drift'. He was buried in Preston Cemetery, and a stone monument was erected to the memory of one of the heroes of Rorkes Drift, 'who was a brave and modest Christian gentleman'.

On his retirement, the Rev Smith settled in Preston and was buried in the Church of England plot of the town's New Hall Lane cemetery.

WALTER ALPHONSUS DUNNE was born on 10th February 1853, in Cork, and **LOUIS ALEXANDER BYRNE** was also born in Ireland in 1857. His father Richard became a prominent ship-owner and merchant after the family had moved to Wales. Dunne served with the Commissariat Department in Dublin from 1873 until 1877, before being posted to South Africa.

For their conduct at Rorke's Drift, Walter Dunne and Louis Byrne were mentioned in despatches. Byrne's name appears on the monument at Rorke's Drift, and his brother Alfred collected his effects. Dunne took part in the re-invasion as a Deputy Commissary.

He was again involved in a siege during the Transvaal war of 1880-81, and like Chaplain Smith, he was present at the battle of Tel-el-Kebir in 1882, and took part in the campaign against the Dervishes. He completed most of his service on the African

Below: *Walter Dunne was the senior Commissariat Officer at Rorke's Drift. He and his fellow officers played a vital part in the organisation and construction of the barricade. He served the British Army for 35 distinguished years.*

Above: *Louis Byrne was twenty-two years old when he was killed in action at Rorke's Drift. For some reason he was buried just outside the little cemetery, but his name appears on the monument.*

Continent and was transferred to the Army Service Corps as a Lieutenant-Colonel in 1888. He was appointed CB in 1896, and was promoted to Colonel in 1897. After thirty-five distinguished years, he retired from the service in Gibraltar in February 1908. He died at The English Nursing Home in Rome on 2nd July 1908.

JAMES LANGLEY DALTON was born in the parish of St Andrews, London. He left his job as a stationer's lad to enlist into the 85th Regt, at Victoria, London, on 20th November 1849. He gave his age as 17 years 11 months, but he was probably younger.

He served his first six months in Ireland, and was then in England, before being posted to Mauritius in 1853. Dalton was a good soldier, and he left the island three years later as a Sergeant. He then went to the Cape to take part in the 8th Frontier War. He was back in England when he was transferred to the Commissariat Staff Corps in 1862, becoming a Colour-Sergeant in June of the following year. He attended the School of Musketry at Hythe in Kent, and was stationed in Aldershot until 1867, becoming a clerk and Master Sergeant. His final tour of overseas duty was in Canada from 1868 until 1871, and while he was there he was transferred to the Army Service Corps, eventually becoming a 1st Class SSGT. He took his discharge in London on 20th November 1871, and was awarded the Long Service Good Conduct Medal.

Below: *James Dalton's excellent initiative and gallantry at Rorke's Drift earned him the praise of several fellow defenders in their subsequent reports on the action.*

Above: *The memorial at the grave of James Langley Dalton VC, at the Russell Road cemetery, Port Elizabeth. In recent years the cemetery has been plagued by vandals.*

He went to South Africa, and volunteered for the appointment of Acting Assistant Commissary on 13th December 1877, when troops were being prepared for the 9th Frontier War. For his conduct at Rorke's Drift, he was mentioned in despatches, and was awarded the Victoria Cross. He was on sick leave for six months after the defence. He then became senior Commissariat Officer at Fort Napier. He received his VC from Major-General Clifford at a ceremony on 16th January 1880. He was given a permanent commission as Sub-Assistant Commissary, and was promoted to Assistant Commissary three weeks later. He was also awarded the South Africa Medal of 1877, with bars for service in 1878 and 1879. He sailed for England in February 1880. It is believed that he served as a volunteer in Egypt, before returning to South Africa in 1884 to try his hand at gold mining in the Transvaal.

He went to stay with his old friend, ex-Sgt John Sherwood Williams, at the Grosvenor Hotel, Port Elizabeth, just before Christmas 1886. After spending the 7th January 1887 in bed, he died suddenly during the night. He was given a quiet civilian burial in the Russell Road Roman Catholic Cemetery, and a memorial was erected in memory of a defender of Rorke's Drift, by Sgt Williams and friends of Natal.

His medals came up for auction at Spink & Son, on 26th September 1986. They had been part of the estate of the late David Spink, who had bought the Victoria Cross in 1949. The Royal Corps of Transport Medal Trust purchased the medal set for £62,000.

FRANCIS ATTWOOD was awarded the silver medal for Distinguished Conduct, and was promoted to Sergeant. He received the medal at a special parade on 13th November 1879.

On his return to England, Francis Attwood married, and served with the Commissariat and Transport Corps at Plymouth. He died suddenly at his home there, on 20th February 1884, aged 38. His medals are on display at The Royal Corps of Transport Museum.

Right: *The Distinguished Conduct Medal and South Africa Medal awarded to Cpl Attwood, now in the Royal Corps of Transport Museum.*
Below: *Cpl Francis Attwood, DCM, was posted in the storehouse during the attack, where he shot down several Zulus who were trying to fire the roof.*

JAMES HENRY REYNOLDS was born on 3rd February 1844, at the inland sea port of Dun Laoghaire, County Dublin, which at the time was called Kingstown. He was the son of Laurence Reynolds JP, of Dalyston House, Granard, County Longford. He was educated at Castle Knock and Trinity College, Dublin, where he graduated BA MB ChB in 1867.

On 31st March 1868 he entered the Medical Staff Corps as an Assistant Surgeon, and joined the 36th (Hereford) Regt as Medical Officer on 24th March 1869. For his efficient service during an outbreak of cholera in the regiment while it was in India, he received a commendation from the Commander-in-Chief, General Lord Sandhurst, and was promoted to Surgeon in 1873.

He served throughout the Zulu War, and for his conduct at Rorke's Drift, he was mentioned in despatches, and was awarded the Victoria Cross. He received his medal from Lord Wolseley during a special parade at St Paul's, Zululand, on 16th July

James Reynolds was promoted to Surgeon-Major after the defence. He died in London in 1932 and was buried in St Mary's cemetery, where several VC recipients are laid to rest.

Late Victorian medical attention 1884-98. A typical scene of the day. A corporal of the Medical Staff Corps looks on as the army doctor examines soldiers.

1879. He was given special promotion to Surgeon-Major, dated 23rd January 1879, and was elected honorary Fellow of the Royal College of Physicians of Ireland; and made honorary Doctor of Law, Dublin. He was awarded a gold medal by the British Medical Association in July 1879.

He married his wife Elizabeth in 1880. He was a keen all-round sportsman, and was a member of the Army and Navy Club from 1890 until his death. He was promoted to Lieutenant-Colonel in 1887, and to Brigade-Surgeon Lieutenant-Colonel in 1892. He retired in 1896, and became senior medical officer at the Royal Army Clothing Factory at Pimlico in London. On 9th November 1929, he and John Williams VC were among the guests of honour at a VCs' dinner given by the Prince of Wales in the House of Lords.

He died at the Empire Nursing Home, Victoria, London, on 4th March 1932, and is buried in the north-east corner of Kensal Green Roman Catholic Cemetery, Harrow Road, London. Grave number is 504. A black stone cross marks the spot.

On the day after the battle Doctor Reynolds stated: 'I am glad to say that the men of AHC behaved splendidly.' For his conduct at Rorke's Drift, 2nd Cpl Michael McMahon AHC was mentioned in despatches, and on the 15th January 1880 he was recommended for the Distinguished Conduct Medal. But this was cancelled two weeks later for going absent without leave and stealing certain items.

GONVILLE BROMHEAD was born at Versailles in France, on 29th August 1845. He was the third son of Edmund de Gonville Bromhead, 3rd Baronet. He was a landowner, who had been a Lieutenant at Waterloo, and had retired from the army as a Major. The family home was at Thurlby Hall, Newark-on-Trent, Notttinghamshire, and he was educated at Magnus Grammar School there. He enjoyed sports, and was a good left-hand medium bowler in their successful cricket eleven.

He entered the 24th Regt as an Ensign by purchase, on 20th April 1867. He was tutored at Croydon, where he was popular among his fellow soldiers, and was always ready to offer help to new recruits. While he was there he was the champion at boxing, wrestling and singlestick. He was 5 ft 10 inches tall, and carried a strong broad frame. He was promoted by selection to Lieutenant, on 28th October 1871.

He served in the 9th Frontier War, and for his conduct at Rorke's Drift he was mentioned in despatches and was awarded the Victoria Cross. He was also promoted to Captain, and Brevet-Major dated 23rd January 1879. Just before the re-invasion he moved to Utrecht in the Transvaal, where he received his medal from Lord Wolseley on 22nd August 1879. He also received a South Africa medal with clasp (1877-78-79). He was then posted to Gibraltar.

On 25th June 1880, at a special banquet at Lincoln Masonic Hall, he was presented with an illuminated address and a jewelled dress sword on behalf of the people of Lincoln. In his acceptance speech he mentioned Major Chard, Surgeon-Major Reynolds, Mr Dalton, Mr Dunne, and Rev Smith. The tenants of Thurlby Hall gave him a revolver and Queen Victoria presented him with a picture of herself.

He was posted to the East Indies until March 1881 and on his return home, in 1882, he spent two months at the Hythe School of Musketry, where he gained a First Class Extra certificate. He then joined the South Wales Borderers at Secunderabad in India. He was promoted to Major on 4th April 1883, and served in the Burmese Expedition 1886-88. (Medal with clasps 'Burma 1885-87 & Burma 1887-89'). He then moved back to the East Indies.

He never married, and he died of enteric (typhoid) fever, at Camp Dabhaura, Allahabad, India, on 9th February 1891. His awards and mementos were left to his brother Charles, and his

Major Gonville Bromhead was the only officer of the 24th Regt present at the battle for Rorke's Drift. Upon his return to England he finally attended upon Queen Victoria when this photograph was taken.

Victoria Cross was presented to the Regimental Museum in 1973. His name is inscribed on the colour-pole of the 24th Regiment, and his portrait and uniform can be seen on display in the old Magnus Grammar School building, which is now Newark's Appletongate Museum.

Right: *After the Zulu War, Gonville Bromhead served in Gibraltar, the East Indies and England before being posted to India. Following further service in Burma and the East Indies, he died in India in 1891.*

Below: *A contemporary view of the old Magnus Grammar School at Newark. It was here that Bromhead was educated and the building now houses the Appletongate Museum which contains his uniform.*

THE NATAL MOUNTED POLICE. The first man was enrolled into the police on 12th March 1874. **SYDNEY H. HUNTER** was born in September 1856, and **HENRY LUGG** at Okehampton in Devon in 1859. Lugg had come out from England with Edward and Henry Camp whose sister, Mary, Lugg was courting. They all joined the police at Pietermaritzburg, on 22nd May 1878. **ROBERT S. GREEN** had also enrolled in the capital on 31st August 1877. His father worked in Cape Town, and his brother Harold was also in the police.

Hunter's name appears on the monument at Rorke's Drift, and Green was discharged on 30th April 1881. Harry Lugg was sent to Greys Hospital in Pietermaritzburg with an attack of rheumatic fever, and was discharged as physically infirm for further service on 28th February 1879. Later he became District Adjutant to the Natal Volunteers and magistrate of Umsinga.

Right: *The information shown on this death certificate is all that is known about Sydney Hunter, the mounted policeman killed at Rorke's Drift.*

Above: *The Natal Mounted Police on their way to the front. Under Major John Dartnell, a veteran of the Indian Mutiny, they were a well-trained unit.*

Right: *This section taken from the enlistment register of the Natal Mounted Police at the time of the Zulu War, gives details about R. Green and his brother.*

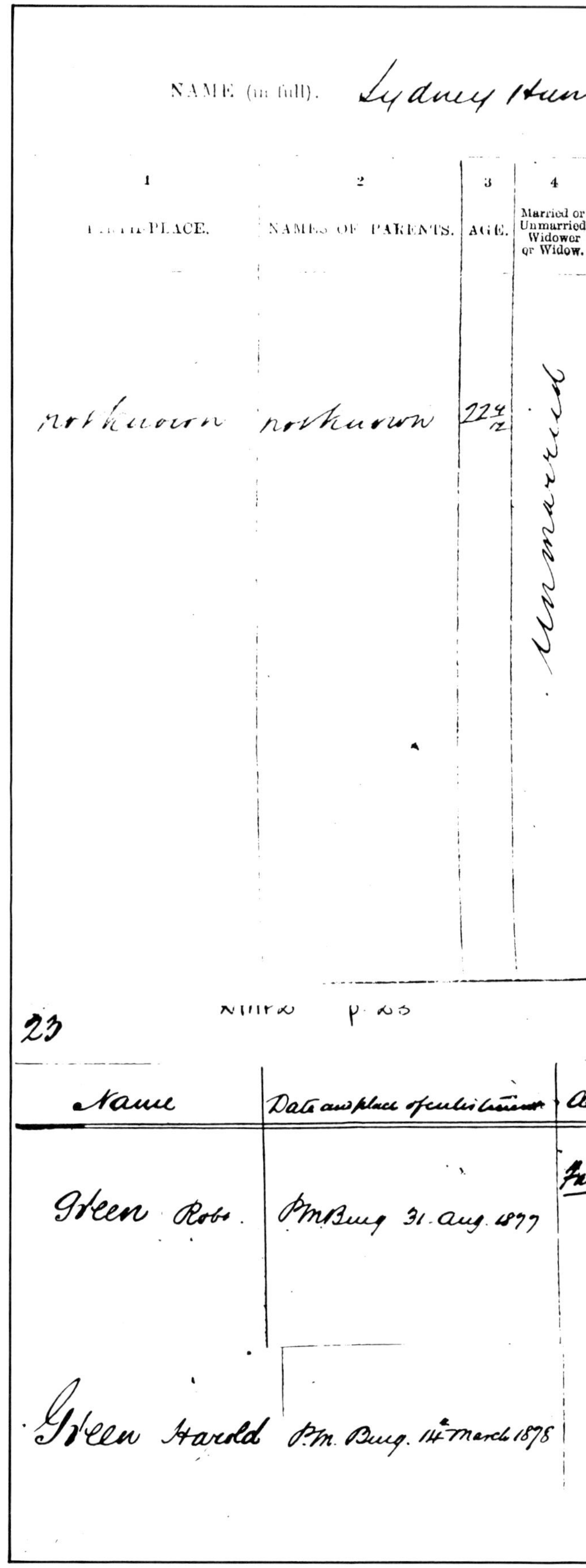

NAME (in full). Sydney Hun

1 BIRTHPLACE.	2 NAMES OF PARENTS.	3 AGE.	4 Married or Unmarried, Widower or Widow.
not known	not known	22 4/12	Unmarried

23

Name	Date and place of enlistment
Green Robt.	PMBurg 31. Aug. 1877
Green Harold	P.M. Burg. 14th March 1878

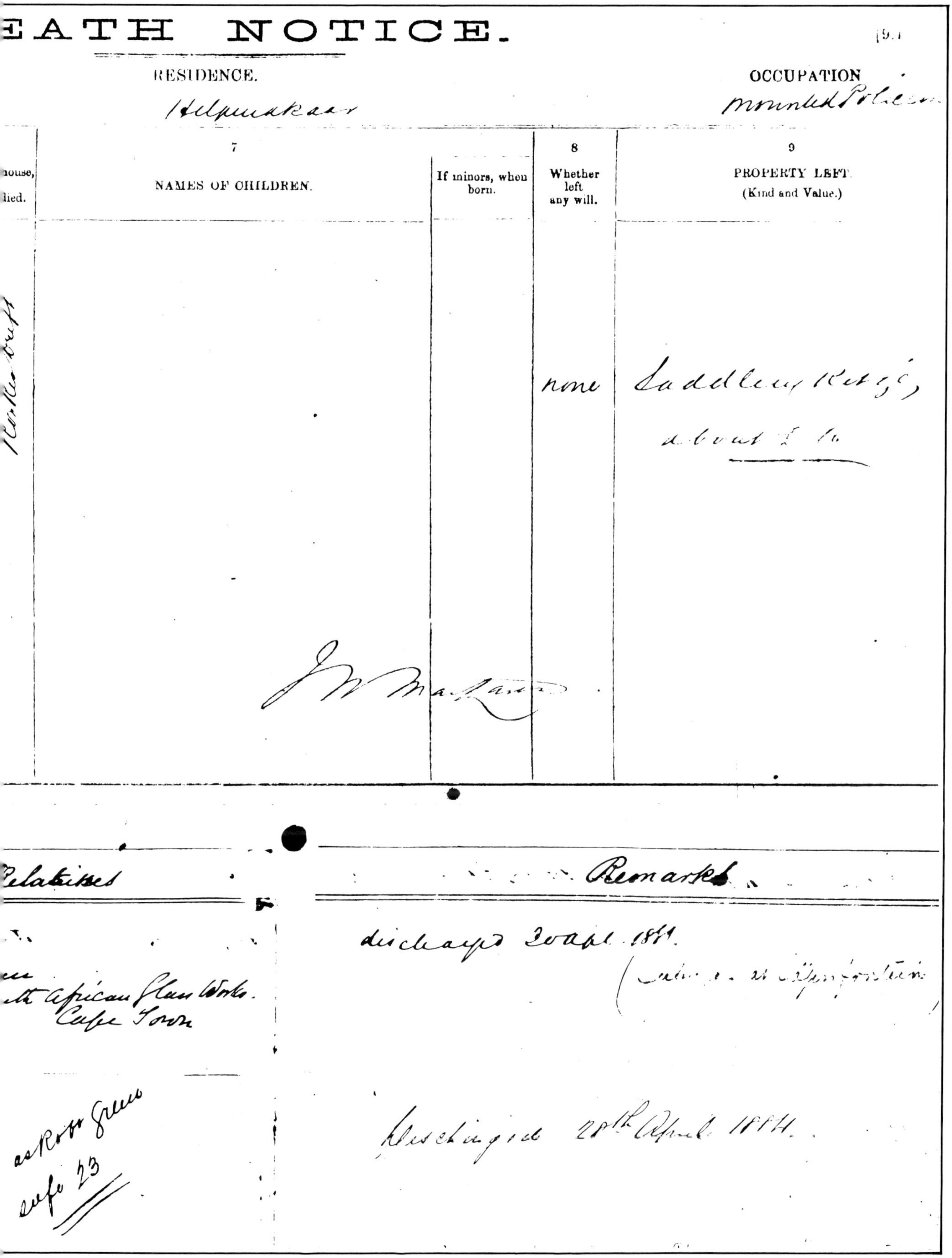
EATH NOTICE.

RESIDENCE. Helpmakaar

OCCUPATION Mounted Police

louse, lied.	7 NAMES OF CHILDREN.	If minors, when born.	8 Whether left any will.	9 PROPERTY LEFT. (Kind and Value.)
Rorkes Drift			none	Saddlery &c, about £ 6

Relatives

th African Glass Works. Cape Town

Remarks

discharged 20 Apl. 1881.

Discharged 20th April 1884.

2985 / 84

P. M. Burg, 2nd August, 1884.

To
Colonel Mitchel
Colonial Secretary
P. M. Burg.

Honored Sir

I venture to address your Honor once more for the purpose of getting your valuable assistance in obtaining some employment for me in the Government service as you will see by the attached letter from Mr. Hunter, Genl. Manager N.G.Ry that there is not the slightest chanse to get employed on the Railway at the present time.

I would regard it as an act of great favor, if you would kindly recomend me to the Superintendent of the Govt. Prisons to enable me to get employed as turnkey or anything else in that branch of the service. in fact any situation in any other Dept. of the Govt. service would suite me, no matter how small the salary will be.

Trusting you will be good enough to give this application your favorible consilderation

I remain
Honored Sir
very respectfully
Your obedient servant
F. C. Schiess
Ex Post Master
P. M. Burg.

CORPORAL SCHIESS preferred to be called Friedrich, but his real names were Ferdnand Christian.

He was born at Bergedorf, Berne, in Switzerland, on 7th April 1856. He was brought up in an orphanage, and at the age of fifteen he served on the side of France in the Franco-Prussian War. He then went to South Africa.

For his conduct at Rorke's Drift he was mentioned in despatches, and became the first man serving with South African forces, under British command, to be awarded the Victoria Cross. Wearing the green uniform of Lonsdale's Horse, he received the medal from Lord Wolseley, at a parade of the troops in the market square in Pietermaritzburg, on 3rd February 1880. Schiess was a shy man and he soon took the medal off. But he enjoyed the rest of the day being driven round the town in an open carriage.

At that time he was employed in the telegraph office at Durban. But by 1884 he had fallen on hard times, and was desperately applying for government work in Pietermaritzburg. But he was unsuccessful. He was offered a passage to England aboard the troop-ship *Serapis*, the cost of his rations being paid for by a public fund. But he was too ill to survive such a trip, and he died on 14th December 1884. He was buried at sea off the coast of Angola, Southern Africa.

Schiess could speak and write good English, and it was only discovered that he was a Swiss national after his death. Even though he was destitute he did not part with his Victoria Cross. It was brought to England, and after spending some years locked away in a drawer at the War Office, it is now in the display at The National Army Museum, London.

A strange note appears at the back of a page in Capt Penn-Symons's report at Brecon. It states: 'I saw Corp. Schiess in Nov. 1891, in Allahabad, India. He had been working in a jeweller's shop, and was just going to Australia. Being afraid to lose his Victoria Cross, he has sent it on ahead by registered post to his destination.'

Left: *This application for employment was written by Corporal Schiess shortly before his death. The reply was: 'Inform applicant that there is very little chance for him.' One of the heroes who had saved South Africa from: '. . . the darkest cloud of invasion', was unable to gain employment there. He died in utter destitution at the age of 28.*

Above: *Although Corporal Schiess became destitute he retained possession of his Victoria Cross, and when he died on board the* Serapis *the medal was found on his body. It was shipped to England and ended up at the War Office. It has now found a permanent home in the National Army Museum.*

JOHN ROUSE MERRIOTT CHARD was born at Boxhill, near Plymouth, on 21st December 1847. He was the second son of William Chard, who came from Pathe, Othery, in Somerset. He was educated at Plymouth New Grammar School, at Cheltenham College, and passed out of the Royal Military Academy at Woolwich as a Lieutenant in the Royal Engineers on 15th July 1868.

He served for two years at Chatham, three years in Bermuda, and one year in Malta. Then after three more years in southern England, he boarded the *Teuton* at Plymouth on 2nd December 1878 to sail to the Cape. He arrived in Durban on 4th January 1879.

For his conduct at Rorke's Drift he was awarded the Victoria Cross, and was promoted Captain, and Brevet-Major, dated 23rd January 1879. He received the medal from Lord Wolseley, at a parade of the troops at St Paul's, Zululand, on 16th July 1879.

He returned to a hero's welcome. The people of Plymouth presented him with a sword of honour and a gold chronometer watch. And he received an illuminated address from the St George's Lodge of Freemasons in Exeter. John Chard was an unassuming man and a likeable soldier. But he seems to have been a person who took life as it came, with no particular ambition. However, Queen Victoria was fond of him, and he was invited to an audience with her on several occasions.

He served at Devonport, in Cyprus and in India, with postings at home depots in Chatham, Preston and Cardiff in between. He was made substantive Major in 1886, and was promoted to Lieutenant-Colonel on 8th January 1893, while he was in Singapore. On 8th January 1896, he was promoted to Colonel, and appointed commanding Royal Engineer at the sub-district of Perth, Scotland.

He was attacked by cancer of the tongue, and was too ill to go to Balmoral on the Queen's invitation in November 1896. He missed attending the Queen's jubilee celebrations in 1897. But on 11th July he received a Jubilee Medal from her, and a signed portrait. He went to Edinburgh three times for operations to remove his tongue, and although he was still able to speak, his condition became worse, and he was placed on sick leave from 8th August 1897. He suffered much distress towards the end, and he died at his younger brother Charles's rectory of St John the Baptist, in Hatch Beauchamp, near Taunton, on the evening of 1st November 1897. Being such a travelled man he had never married.

Lt John Chard VC was promoted Brevet-Major and returned to a hero's welcome in England. He received several presentations, including some from Queen Victoria, who invited him to an audience with her on several occasions. He was a handsome and modest man. He suffered a painful death when he was fifty, struck down by cancer of the tongue.

He was buried in the churchyard there with military honours. The Duke of Connaught, who had been with him as a young officer at Woolwich, sent a letter of sympathy, as did Lord Chelmsford. Queen Victoria had shown much concern about him, and had enquired about his condition throughout his illness. She sent a laurel wreath to his funeral with the inscription: 'A mark of admiration and regard for a brave soldier, from his sovereign.' This tribute – and an anonymous wreath bearing the inscription: 'In remembrance of Rorke's Drift, 22nd January 1879 – That day he did his duty' were

Above: *Sir Garnet Wolseley decorates Major Chard at St Paul's, Zululand, on 16 July 1879, when a number of awards were presented, including the VC to Surgeon-Major Reynolds. Fate seems to have placed Chard in command at Rorke's Drift, and by 3 o'clock on 22 January 1879 he was destined to become a national hero.*

placed on the coffin. There were wreaths from Sir Bartle-Frere's widow, Colonel Bourne and the officers of the South Wales Borderers; and Colonel Walter Dunne, A.A.G. York. A marble cross is the memorial to the hero of Rorke's Drift.

A memorial window was placed in Hatch Beauchamp church; there is a memorial to him in Rochester Cathedral; and he is the subject of a bronze bust in the Shire Hall at Taunton – which is a replica of one in The Royal Engineers' Museum, Chatham. His name is inscribed on the colour-pole of the 24th Regt, and on the Roll of Honour, Big

Above: 'In Memoriam – Colonel J.R.M. Chard VC, RE, died 1st Nov. 1897'. The window in Hatch Beauchamp Church is one of the memorials that have been erected in honour of his name.

Classical, Cheltenham College. There is still a John Chard decoration awarded to the South African Defence Force.

The whereabouts of his original Victoria Cross are not known, but his family has a replica.

FRANK BOURNE was born in the village of Balcombe, near Crawley in Sussex, on 27th April 1854. He was the youngest of eight sons in a farming family. He enlisted against his father's wishes, at Reigate, on 18th December 1872. He was 5 feet 6 inches tall, with a dark complexion, grey eyes and brown hair.

He was promoted to Corporal on 11th April 1875 and, shortly after arriving in South Africa, he was promoted three times in as many weeks – finally becoming Colour-Sergeant on 27th April 1878. He served in the Frontier War, and for his conduct at Rorke's Drift he was mentioned in despatches, and in July 1879, he was awarded the Distinguished Conduct Medal, with an annuity of ten pounds. He was also offered a commission, but he did not, at that time, have the finance needed to follow the life of an officer.

He married his wife Eliza in 1882, and had five children. He served in Gibraltar, India and Burma, eventually becoming a Honorary Lieutenant and Quartermaster in 1890. He was then appointed Adjutant at the Hythe School of Musketry until his retirement in 1907. He worked for the Society of Miniature Rifle Clubs in London, and was Adjutant at the Dublin school of Musketry during the Great War. He was promoted to Lieutenant-Colonel, and was awarded the OBE for his services.

The Northern Command Military Tattoo, which was held in Gateshead in 1934, included a sketch acting out the defence. Lt-Col Bourne appeared in the arena with Sgt Saxty and Ptes William Cooper, John Jobbins and Caleb Woods, who were also survivors of the battle. The verse taken from Macaulay's *Lays of Ancient Rome*, which introduces the fourth chapter of this book, was used to present the programme of the tattoo. And Bourne remembered it. On 20th December 1936, he spoke on BBC radio about his experiences in South Africa, and recited this verse to end the programme. He replied personally to the hundreds of letters he received afterwards.

The anniversary of the battle was always celebrated by a family dinner at his home, and for the rest of his life he was proud of the way the men of 'B' Company had behaved on that fateful day. He died on 8th May 1945, possibly the last survivor of the Rorke's Drift garrison, and is buried at Elmers End, Kent.

Right: *Col-Sgt Frank Bourne DCM, was the senior NCO during the defence of Rorke's Drift. He rose to the rank of Lieutenant-Colonel and was awarded the OBE during his long and distinguished career. When he died in Beckenham at the grand old age of 91, he was the last known survivor of the Rorke's Drift garrison.*

Below: *Although no official Rorke's Drift commemoration society came into being, many of the surviving defenders kept in touch. This is the front cover of the programme for the Gateshead Military Tattoo in 1934, where five survivors appeared in the arena to act out the progressive stages of the battle.*

ALFRED HENRY HOOK, or 'Harry' as he preferred to be called, was born at Alney, Churcham, near Gloucester, on 6th August 1850. His father was a farmer. He served in the Monmouth Militia for five years, whilst living in Drybridge Street, Monmouth. He is believed to have married and had a daughter before enlisting at Monmouth on 13th March 1877.

He went with his Battalion to South Africa, and took part in the Frontier War. For his conduct at Rorke's Drift he was mentioned in despatches, and was awarded the Victoria Cross. He was stationed at Rorke's Drift throughout the Zulu War, and at a special parade there on 3rd August, he became one of the very few people to be decorated with the Victoria Cross at the place where he had earned it. Lord Wolseley conducted the ceremony. He also received a Medal for South Africa (clasp 1877-8-9), and a number of Good Conduct and Marksmanship badges. He was then posted to Gibraltar.

He bought himself out of the army for eighteen pounds, on 25th June 1880. When he got home he found that his wife (who may have been only his common-law wife) had sold his property and had remarried because she thought that he had been killed. He moved to Sydenham Hill, London, and at Christmas 1881 he began working for the British museum, eventually becoming a cloakroom attendant in the reading room. He married his wife Ada at Islington in 1897, and lived in Pimlico. He served for twenty years as a Sergeant in the 1st Volunteer Bn of the Royal Fusiliers, and was a well respected member of The Loyal St James Lodge of Oddfellows.

He began to suffer ill-health, and retired on the last day of 1904. He returned to his native county to see if the air would help to combat his condition, and he was welcomed as a popular hero. His Victoria Cross annuity was due to increase to fifty pounds on 1st April 1905, but he did not live to benefit. He died of pulmonary tuberculosis on the morning of 12th March 1905, at 2 Osborne Villas, Roseberry Avenue, Gloucester, leaving his wife and two young daughters. A print of the famous painting 'The Defence of Rorke's Drift' by Alphonse De Neuville, which is reproduced on the cover of this book, was hanging by his head. He had been known as a quiet man who would only talk about the defence in private conversation.

His funeral was a striking spectacle. John Fielding VC sent a message of sympathy, and Fred Hitch attended with his son who, as a Corporal in the South Wales Borderers, was one of the bearers. Twenty-three regiments were represented in all. He was buried with full military honours at Churcham. Eighteen months later a marble cross was unveiled over his grave. 'Erected by admiring civilians and local Regiments, in memory of his heroic share in the defence of Rorke's Drift, Natal, 1879.' His Victoria Cross is now with the Regimental Museum, and there is also a memorial in Brecon Cathedral.

Left: *Alfred Henry Hook of the 24th Regt was presented with his VC at Rorke's Drift in August 1879. A year later he bought himself out of the army and moved to London.*

Below: *Seven members of the 24th Regt, all holders of the VC, gather for a reunion. Of these, six fought in the Zulu War of 1879. Top row, left to right – Robert Jones, 'Harry' Hook, William Jones. Front row – David Bell (awarded VC in 1867), Colonel Edward Browne, Frederick Hitch and John Williams (Fielding).*

Left: *Henry Hook in the uniform of a sergeant in the 1st Volunteer Bn, the Royal Fusiliers with whom he served as a weapons instructor.*

Below: *Henry Hook's funeral cortège, escorted by representatives from twenty-three regiments, moves through Gloucester on the 18 March 1905.*

Sgt Hook's coffin is carried past the guard of honour by the door of Churcham church on the outskirts of Gloucester.

On 22 September 1906, Col Curll of the South Wales Borderers prepares to unveil the memorial over Henry Hook's grave.

FREDERICK HITCH was born in New Southgate, which until 1881 was a borough of Edmonton, Middlesex. He had been a building labourer, and when he attested at Westminster Police Court on 7th March 1877, he could not sign his name on the papers, and his monument records the 2nd November 1856 as the date of his birth. He was 5 feet 9 inches tall, with a fresh complexion, hazel eyes and brown hair.

He took part in the Frontier War, and for his conduct at Rorke's Drift he was awarded the Victoria Cross. After the defence he travelled by ambulance wagon to Durban, and from there was invalided home aboard the *Tamar*. Queen Victoria decorated him personally at Netley Military Hospital, Southampton, on 12th August 1879. A medical board found that his arm had been permanently disabled, and he was invalided from the army on 25th August 1879. He received a medal for South Africa (clasp 1877-8-9).

He went to live in Southgate, where he married his wife Emma in July 1880, and began working for the Corps of Commissionaires, at the Imperial Institute. Cecil Rhodes visited him to congratulate him on his bravery. While he was working at the Royal United Services Institute, Whitehall in 1901, a thief cut his medal from his coat. A replacement was ordered by King Edward VII, which was presented to him in 1908. Some years later one of his sons had to bid £85 at a public auction to buy back the original medal that had been stolen.

He owned a horse-cab and two horses, but when the age of the automobile began to make its mark, he went to work as a taxi-driver for the General Motor Cab Company. After his wife died he lived quietly for the last seven years of his life, in lodgings at 62 Cranbrook Road, Chiswick. Whilst on strike from his job, he died suddenly of pleuro-pneumonia and heart-failure, on the evening of 6th January 1913. He was aged 56 years, and left six grown-up children.

John Fielding VC and Frank Bourne DCM attended his funeral, along with more than a thousand London cabbies. He was buried with full military honours in Chiswick Old Cemetery. A memorial was erected by voluntary subscription, to commemorate his heroic action at Rorke's Drift Among the subscribers was a relative of Col Chard. His Victoria Cross was sold in 1929 and is now with the Regimental museum.

Left: *Pte Frederick Hitch VC, a twenty-two year old North Londoner, was dangerously wounded at Rorke's Drift, and was invalided to Netley Military Hospital, where Queen Victoria presented him with the Victoria Cross.*

Below: *Fred Hitch with his Martini-Henry rifle. His shattered shoulder joint ended his army career, and he returned to London. He worked as a member of the Corps of Commissionaires until acquiring his own horse-cab. He was employed as a London cab-driver when he died suddenly in 1913.*

RETREAT TO HELPMEKAAR. In his 1905 report Pte Hook says: 'Lt Chard rushed up from the river, and saw Lt Bromhead. Orders were given to strike camp and make ready to go, and we actually loaded up two wagons. Then Mr Dalton came up . . .'

Rev Smith states that: 'A praiseworthy effort was made to remove the worst cases in hospital to a place of safety. Two wagons were brought up after some delay, and the patients were being brought out, when it was found that the Zulus were too close . . .'

These statements contradict Chard. In both of his reports he says that the men had already started the barricade when he arrived from the river. Both Bourne and Dunne mention the wagons being brought up to be included in the barricade, but make no reference to their being used in an attempt to evacuate the wounded. In my opinion none was made.

I believe that, when the wagons were being brought up to the barricade, it coincided with the time when the ambulatory patients were leaving the hospital to take their places at the wall. And Rev Smith, who was still on the Oskarberg when the decisions were made, confused this with an effort to remove the sick. And Hook, who would have been occupied with his work within the hospital, mistook the utilisation of the wagons for an attempt to retreat. He makes no mention of an attempt to retreat in his 1891 report, but he is likely to have read Rev Smith's report in *The Historical Records of the Twenty-Fourth Regiment*, and this may have jogged his memory that he had noticed the wagons being brought up, and had simply drawn the same conclusion as Smith.

The outposts of Helpmekaar were situated ten miles from the border with Zululand on the road from Pietermaritzburg to the Buffalo River at Rorke's Drift. It was little more than a clutter of makeshift buildings and corrugated sheds when Lord Chelmsford established his headquarters here, and two companies of the 1st/24th Regiment were posted to guard the supply depot. Luckily, the regimental colour of the 1st Battalion was also left behind at Helpmekaar.

LT ADENDORFF is normally ascribed to be the man who informed Lt Chard about the advancing *impi*. In his official account Chard reported that Lt Adendorff: 'who afterwards remained to assist in the defence', informed him 'of the disaster befallen at the Isandula [sic] camp, and that the Zulus were advancing upon Rorke's Drift.' In the same report he also states that when he got to the store he: 'found that a note had been received from the third column, stating that the enemy was advancing in force against our post.'

However, in a longer account he wrote for Queen Victoria a year later – having had time to think – he makes no mention that Adendorff had informed him of the *impi*, but confirms the reference to the note from the third column and its details. There is evidence that Adendorff left the camp at Isandhlwana very early on, and therefore would not have known about the *impi*.

This means that either Bromhead passed the information to Chard by way of his message, or that Chard was unaware of the danger until he got to the store. The reports suggest that Bromhead sent for Chard as soon as Pte Evans brought the news of the disaster, which was before the note from the third column had arrived. Rev Smith states that Bromhead sent for Chard 'to come up and direct the preparations for defence.' If this was so, Bromhead would also have explained to Chard why it was necessary to do so. But as I have said previously, Rev Smith was still on the Oskarberg with Mr Witt when the reports came in, and in both of his accounts Chard says that the messenger arrived: 'asking me to come up at once', with no warning of the *impi*. Which brings me to the conclusion that Chard had no knowledge of the danger until he got to the mission-station.

There has also been doubt that Lt Adendorff took part in the defence. The suspicion arises from the fact that he was arrested in Pietermaritzburg to face a charge of desertion, and also because he was not known to have been positively recalled during the fighting. But the charge of desertion in the face of the enemy is more likely to have been from the camp at Isandhlwana. No trial is known to have taken place.

In his account to Queen Victoria, Chard makes a reference to Adendorff's being in the store. Pte Hook says that the Lieutenant stayed behind. And a Natal Carbineer called J.P. Symons, who was with the column when it relieved the garrison on the morning of 23rd January, makes a reference in his account to having been told of a German who had been posted in the store. This could also have been Adendorff. Both Chard and Symons state that the man to whom they refer, was responsible for shooting a Zulu who was trying to set light to the roof of the store. This would account for his not being remembered much during the battle. Cpl Attwood, who received a DCM, was also posted in the store and he is not mentioned in any of the reports that I have read.

The Carbineer who was with Adendorff when he arrived at the drift (said to have been a Sgt Vane), is quite positively recorded as riding on to Helpmekaar. Several other fugitives are named by the defenders as having retreated to Helpmekaar, but there is no account stating definitely that Adendorff decamped. His name also appears on a roll of defenders that was put together on 3rd February 1879.

I find it impossible to accept that Lt James Adendorff left Rorke's Drift before the Zulu attack and I believe it would be doing him an injustice if I did not include him in the narrative.

THE EXPERIENCES OF COMBAT and how the men at Rorke's Drift felt, are based on a study of the statements made by the defenders, and the stories told to me by my late grandfather, George Hallam, who was with the Lancashire Fusiliers in the trenches at Ypres during the Great War; and my uncle, James Bancroft, who was with the Highland Light Infantry (City of Glasgow Regt) during several campaigns in the Second World War. Same feelings – whoever the enemy!

'AS BLACK AS HELL AND AS THICK AS GRASS', is a favourite quote from the action, so it is important to ascertain who said it.

Donald Morris states in 'The Washing of the Spears', that it was Pte John Wall, 24th Regt, who used the words to warn the post as he returned from the Oskarberg with the two clerics. But neither Rev Smith nor Rev Witt mention either Wall or the quote in their accounts, and he did not return with Dr Reynolds, if he ever did go up the Oskarberg to begin with.

In his book 'Rorke's Drift', Michael Glover states that it was Pte Hitch who said it, as he slid off the roof of the storehouse. But Hitch says nothing of this in his accounts and I cannot find any evidence to connect Hitch with the quote at all.

Trooper Lugg states in his account that: 'A man named Hall of the RMB rode out to see if he could see anything of them, and on going out about 1,000 yards, he could see them just a mile off, as he described it, "as black as hell and as thick as grass".' This report was written soon after the event.

In a letter to the *Natal Witness*, Robert J. Hall confirms that he was asked to reconnoitre over the hill, and on seeing the Zulus galloped back to the house (where Lugg was posted), remarking: 'The Zulus are upon us.' It is not unlikely to suppose that Hall forgot his exact words spoken in a situation of great excitement, with thousands of Zulu warriors on his heels, when writing about it nearly thirty years later.

Trooper Henry Lugg, seated second from the right on the front row, remained in South Africa in a civilian capacity after the Zulu War. Alphonse de Neuville used Lugg's letters as basic information for his painting, which is reproduced on the cover of this book.

WILLIAM WILSON ALLEN was born in February 1844 at St Andrews, Newcastle-upon-Tyne. He enlisted at York on 27th October 1859, and joined the 24th Regt at Aldershot. He was 5 feet 4 inches tall. During his early career he served on Mauritius, and was confined in cells on several occasions. He re-engaged in 1873 and was posted to the Regimental Depot in 1874, eventually becoming a Corporal on 6th July 1877, and being appointed assistant schoolmaster. He returned to his battalion just in time to go to the Cape.

He took part in the Frontier War, being promoted to Lance-Sergeant in May 1878, but on 21st October 1878, he was reverted back to Corporal. He was also awarded a Good Shooting and Distance Judging Prize in the same year. For his conduct at Rorke's Drift he was awarded the Victoria Cross. He was invalided to Netley, but he was serving at Brecon again by November. The Zulu bullet had left his arm partly disabled.

He received his medal from Queen Victoria, in the lobby at Windsor Castle, on 9th December 1879.

For his conduct at Rorke's Drift, Pte William Roy, a red-haired Scotsman from Edinburgh, was mentioned in despatches, and was presented with the Distinguished Conduct Medal at the same ceremony. But a disease had affected his vision and he had been discharged from the army two days previously. Both men also received the Medal for South Africa (clasp 1877-8-9).

Cpl Allen became provisional Sergeant at Colchester on 11th June 1880, and then in 1886 he was appointed Sergeant, Instructor of Musketry, to 'C' Company, 4th Volunteer Bn, South Wales Borderers at Monmouth, where he became a popular and respected man. His eighth child, Jessie, was born there in the same year but she died before she was two.

In February 1890 an influenza epidemic hit the town and Sgt Allen was a victim. He died on the morning of 12th March 1890, at 85 Monnow Road, Monmouth, leaving his wife, Sara-Ann, and seven children, none of whom had reached their teens. The Mayor of Monmouth set up an appeal to help them. Sgt Allen was buried with full military honours in Monmouth cemetery and the occasion created great interest in the town. A stone cross was later placed over his grave by the Volunteer Bn of the South Wales Borderers. His Victoria Cross was sold in June 1906, and is now in the possession of the Regimental museum.

Corporal William Wilson Allen VC was a small man with a tough 'Geordie' character. He received a wound at Rorke's Drift which left his arm partly disabled, but he was serving the regiment again before the end of the year. He was a good marksman, and used his skill to gain an appointment as an Instructor of Musketry in Monmouth. He succumbed to a serious bout of influenza at the age of 46, leaving seven young children.

ALFRED SAXTY was born at Buckland Dinham, near Frome in Somerset, in 1857. He enlisted at Newport on 11th September 1876. He was 5 feet 7 inches tall, with a fresh complexion, blue eyes and light-brown hair.

He was mentioned in despatches for his conduct in the Frontier War, and was promoted from Corporal to Sergeant after the defence of Rorke's Drift, but he was reverted back to Corporal later. He was promoted and demoted several times during his army career. He moved to Gibraltar and then served in India. He married in Madras in December 1885, and his first child was born there. Then after his wife died he re-engaged into the Bedfordshire Regt on the first day of 1888, to complete twenty-one years. He married his second wife, Mary, at Secunderabad, where his second son was born in 1890. His third son was born at Rangoon, which is where he had moved to after transferring into the 2nd Royal Inniskillin Fusiliers, on 30th November 1891. He was discharged at his own request, at Thayetmayo, Burma, on 28th February 1895, and settled in Rangoon. Some time later he returned to Britain.

He was admitted as an in-pensioner at the Royal Military Hospital, Chelsea, on 12th June 1930, and then made his home with friends in Blewitt Street, Newport. Early in 1936 he suffered a stroke and was moved to Woolaston House Infirmary Newport, as a private patient. He died there on 11th July 1936, of myocarditis and senility, and was buried in the Roman Catholic section of Newport cemetery, with full military honours. Lt-Col Bourne and five other survivors of the Rorke's Drift garrison sent a wreath, although two of the names – Owen and Thomas – may not have actually taken part in the defence. Pte John Lawton, aged eighty-six, who was with Lord Chelmsford's relief column, insisted on walking with the cortège as a mark of respect.

THE DESCRIPTION OF THE EVENTS WITHIN THE HOSPITAL is based on the points below. The figures tally if it is accepted that Pte Waters was counted as one of the sick, and there is much evidence to suggest this.

Before the news of the Isandhlwana disaster reached Rorke's Drift there were thirty-six patients in the hospital. When Lt Purvis left there were thirty-five, but thirty-six men including Waters.

Pte W. Jones stated in his account that there were twenty-three sick men in the hospital during the struggle and three of these were left behind when he got out. The only three men whom he could have witnessed were Sgt Maxfield and Ptes Beckett and Waters. Thus Pte Waters was counted as a patient in his number of the sick.

In the London Gazette VC citations it states that John Williams and two patients got out of the first hole. In Pte Hook's 1891 account, he says that he retired to a room where there was a number of sick – 'for a few moments I was the only fighting man there. A wounded man of the 24th came to me from another room with a bullet wound in the arm. I tied it up. Then John Williams came in . . .' This was undoubtedly Pte Waters, who was the only man to receive such a wound in the vicinity of the hospital. In an interview on his return to England, Pte Waters stated: 'I saw Pte Horrigan killed.' For Waters to have witnessed Pte Horrigan's plight he must have been in the vicinity of the first escape hole, and Horrigan must have been one of the two patients who escaped with John Williams. In his account, Rev Smith states that Pte Jenkins was seized and dragged away as he ventured through an escape hole. But Lt Chard makes a reference to Pte Jenkins fighting close to him. It seems certain that Rev Smith meant Horrigan, both men being from the 1st Bn.

In his 1905 account Hook states: 'In the room where I now was, there were nine sick men, and I

'Lest We Forget': Pte Joseph Williams and Pte William Horrigan hold back the Zulu horde with rifle fire, in a desperate attempt to give John Williams time to cut a hole in the partition. They fought hard, but both men were soon to die at the hands of frenzied warriors. Their names are among those recorded on the monument at Rorke's Drift. Of the two defenders and four patients who were trapped in this room when the Zulus attacked the hospital only John Williams survived.

was alone to look after them for some time. Suddenly in the thick smoke I saw John Williams . . .' Pte Waters was thus one of these nine, as he was already in the room before Williams and his surviving patient entered. This also confirms the VC citation that Hook and Williams had rescued eight patients. Ten patients got through the second escape hole and in his interview Pte Waters said that he and Pte Beckett had not got through the third hole.

Finally, the VC citations state that the Joneses got six patients out through the window, Sgt Maxfield being left behind, and a number of accounts refer to Trooper Hunter being killed as he struggled to get to the entrenchment. Reports state that five corpses had burned in the hospital – Adams, Hayden, Horrigan, Maxfield and the native. And a medical report states that seven patients had been killed during the struggle to escape from the building – add Beckett and Hunter.

JOHN FIELDING was born in Merthyr Road, Abergavenny, on 24th May 1857. He was one of eight children. The family moved to Cwmbran when John was five. He went to work in the Patent Nut and Bolt Factory in 1865, but after being in the Monmouthshire Militia, he enlisted at Monmouth on 22nd May 1877. His father disapproved, so he used the name Williams so as not be traced.

He went with his Battalion to South Africa and took part in the Frontier War. For his conduct at Rorke's Drift he was mentioned in despatches, and was awarded the Victoria Cross. He moved to Gibraltar where he received the medal from Major-General Anderson on the Almeda Parade Ground,

on 1st March 1880. He also received a medal for South Africa (clasp 1877-8-9). The action is said to have turned his hair white overnight.

He was posted to India, and returned home from Secunderabad in October 1883. He was transferred to the army reserve, becoming a sergeant in the 3rd Volunteer Bn, South Wales Borderers. He was discharged from this unit on 22nd May 1893, and was attached to the civilian staff at Brecon until his retirement on 20th May 1920. His eldest son, Tom, had been killed whilst serving with the South Wales Borderers in the Great War.

On 26th June 1920, he attended a garden party for holders of the VC, given by King George V and Queen Mary at Buckingham Palace. He also attended the VC dinner in 1929 with Reynolds.

After his wife Elizabeth died, he went to live with his daughter at 28 Cocker Avenue, Cwmbran. On 24th November 1932, he took his daily walk to the house of his other daughter at Tycoch. Whilst there he became ill and died of heart failure on the following morning. He left four grown-up children.

His impressive funeral cortège was half-a-mile long, and there was a place of honour in the procession for survivors of the Zulu War. Among them

Left: *John Fielding VC enlisted under the name of Williams because he did not want to be traced. He served with The South Wales Borderers until 1920. As a result of the horrific experience he went through in the hospital at Rorke's Drift his hair went white while he was still a young man.*

Below: *On 26 June 1920 John Fielding was among the 324 holders of the Victoria Cross who marched to Buckingham Palace to attend the first reunion garden party as guests of King George V and Queen Mary. Here, members of the royal family and the military look on as he is presented to the Queen.*

was John Jobbins who lived in the nearby village of Pontnewynydd. Relatives of Fred Hitch and Harry Hook sent floral tributes, as did Colonel Bourne and the survivors of the Rorke's Drift garrison. He was buried with full military honours in St Michael's Roman Catholic Churchyard, Llantarnum. Later the South Wales Borderers erected a gravestone to his memory and a residential home for the mentally handicapped in Llantarnum was named after him. His Victoria Cross is with the Regimental Museum.

Pte Joseph Williams had worked at the Cordes Dos Works in Newport, prior to enlisting at Monmouth on the day after John Williams, and they were posted to the battalion together. He is mentioned in the citations for the VC awards to Hook and Williams, and his name appears on the monument at Rorke's Drift. It is almost certain that he would have received the VC himself if he had survived, and it is perhaps an injustice that he was overlooked when the rules for the award were changed in 1907.

Pte William Jones VC was discharged in 1880 with chronic rheumatism. He appeared at 'Hamilton's Pansterorama' in Rochdale Civic Hall during the 1880s, and in 1887/88 he toured with Buffalo Bill Cody. But by 1893 he was destitute and was forced to sell his Victoria Cross.

WILLIAM JONES was born in 1839, probably in Evesham, Worcestershire, but possibly in Bristol. His father, James, was in the building trade and he worked in the footwear business before enlisting in Birmingham on 21st December 1858. He was 5 feet 5 inches tall and had a sallow complexion, with brown eyes and hair.

He served on Mauritius, where he was promoted to Corporal in 1859, but he was reduced to Private on 4th September 1860. He then went to Burma where he re-engaged at Rangoon on 10th January 1868. He sailed with his battalion to South Africa and his wife, Elizabeth, went with him. While he was serving in the Frontier War she became ill in childbirth, and he obtained leave to look after her. He worked at repairing footwear to pay for a few comforts for her before she died. He returned to his regiment immediately after her burial.

For his conduct at Rorke's Drift he was mentioned in despatches, and was awarded the Victoria Cross. He was found to be suffering from chronic rheumatism in September 1879, and was invalided to England. He was invited to Windsor Castle, and on 13th January 1880, Queen Victoria decorated him in the lobby there. He was discharged from Netley on 2nd February 1880, as unfit for further service and he went to live in Birmingham.

He re-married, and with the five children he had from his first marriage, he moved to Rutland Street, Chorlton-on-Medlock, Manchester. He toured with Buffalo Bill's Wild West Show in the 1880s and occasionally appeared on the theatre stage in Rochdale to recite an account of the defence. Sadly, he eventually hit on hard times and he was forced to pawn his VC for five pounds in 1893 to feed his family, and then he had to sell the pawn ticket. He began to suffer ill health towards the end of his life. His mind would wander and he began to have nightmares that the Zulus were going to attack. He sometimes took his grand-daughter from her bed and would leave the house in the middle of the night with her in his arms. In 1912 an impoverished old man with a white goatee beard was found wandering the streets, and had to be collected from Bridge Street Workhouse.

He died at the house of his daughter, 6 Brampton Street, Ardwick, on the evening of 15th April 1913,

The resting place of a Rorke's Drift hero in a Manchester cemetery. The 'VC' engraving was added in 1983 but the plot has since grown over. Manchester Council have repeatedly turned down requests to place a suitable memorial at his grave.

leaving his wife, Elizabeth, and seven children. A large crowd witnessed his funeral cortège as it made its way to Philips Park cemetery, Bradford, Manchester, where he was buried with full military honours. The helmet that he wore during the defence had been placed on the coffin. His family were poor at that time and he was put in a public grave, with no mention of his Victoria Cross. But this was put right in 1983, and in 1985 a plaque was put on the wall of the cemetery church to commemorate his burial. His VC turned up in Preston in the 1930s and his family tried to buy it back. It is now with the Regimental museum.

ROBERT JONES, a Welsh country boy, was born at Clytha, near Raglan in Monmouthshire, on 19th August 1857. He was a farm labourer like his father, who was displeased when, on 10th January 1876, he enlisted at Monmouth. He was 5 feet 7½ inches tall, with a fresh complexion, grey eyes and brown hair.

He served in the Frontier War, and for his conduct at Rorke's Drift he was mentioned in despatches, and was awarded the Victoria Cross. He received the medal from Lord Wolseley at Utrecht on 11th September 1879. His service in South Africa left him with one bullet and four assegai wounds. He also received a medal for South Africa (clasp 1877-78-79).

He moved to Gibraltar and then served at Secunderabad, India, 1880-81, before returning to the depot at Brecon. He married at Llantilio in January 1885. He had been transferred to the army reserve in 1883, and after being recalled, he was discharged from the army reserve on 26th January 1888.

He went with his family to live at Peterchurch, near Hereford, where he worked as a labourer for a retired Major. He owned a piece of land in the nearby village of St Margaret's. He had been wounded close to his eyes and this sometimes caused him to have pains in the head. In August 1898 he collapsed at work and was never the same person again. On the morning of 6th September 1898 his wife, Elizabeth, noticed him acting wildly before going to work. When he got there he borrowed the Major's gun and two cartridges and walked off into the garden. He was never seen alive again. Next day a jury decided that he had been temporarily insane, and returned a verdict of suicide while of unsound mind.

He was a good father to his five children and he had been a talented amateur poet. He was given a modest military funeral, and some members of his old regiment brought a beautiful wreath. A fine marble headstone marks the place where he was buried in St Peter's churchyard. His Victoria Cross is the only one of 'B' Company that is still in the hands of a private collector.

Pte Robert Jones VC never really escaped from Rorke's Drift and died in tragic circumstances. On 6 September 1898, aged 41, he placed the muzzle of a loaded rifle in his mouth and pulled the trigger.

JOHN CANTWELL was born in Dublin in 1845. He enlisted into the 9th (Norfolk) Regt in November 1868, and was transferred to the Royal Artillery in 1872. He joined the 5th Brigade in July 1877 and arrived at the Cape with it in January 1878. He was promoted to Bombardier Wheeler in July 1878, but he was reverted to Gunner on the day before the defence. For his conduct at Rorke's Drift he was awarded the Distinguished Conduct Medal in February 1880. He was discharged from Woolwich on 19th July 1889 as medically unfit and went to live in Natal. The whereabouts of his medal is not known.

APPENDIX A

Decorations Awarded to the Defenders of Rorke's Drift

VICTORIA CROSS

Royal Engineers
Lt John Rouse Merriott Chard

24th (2nd Warwickshire) Regt
Lt Gonville Bromhead
1240 Cpl William Wilson Allen
1362 Pte Frederick Hitch
1373 Pte Alfred Henry Hook
716 Pte Robert Jones
593 Pte William Jones
1393 Pte John Williams

Army Medical Department
Surgeon James Henry Reynolds BA MB ChB (Dublin)

Commissariat and Transport Department
Assistant Commissariat Officer James Langley Dalton

Natal Native Contingent
Cpl Ferdnand Christian Schiess

DISTINGUISHED CONDUCT MEDAL

24th (2nd Warwickshire) Regt
2459 Colour-Sgt Frank Bourne
1542 Pte William Roy

Royal Horse Artillery
2076 Gunner John Cantwell

Army Service Corps
24692 2nd Cpl Francis Attwood

APPENDIX B

Casualties at Rorke's Drift

According to the official figures there were twenty-five casualties. But the medical report of twenty-seven is more likely. And many men had slight wounds that were not officially reported.

1st Battalion, 24th Regiment

1861	**Pte William Horrigan**	**killed in action**
841	**Pte James Jenkins**	**killed in action**
625	**Pte Edward Nicholson**	**killed in action**
135	**Pte William Beckett**	**died of wounds**
568	**Pte Patrick Desmond**	**slightly wounded**
447	**Pte John Waters**	**severely wounded**

2nd Battalion, 24th Regiment

623	**Sgt Robert Maxfield**	**killed in action**
987	**Pte John Adams**	**killed in action**
1335	**Pte James Chick**	**killed in action**
801	**Pte Thomas Cole**	**killed in action**
969	**Pte John Fagan**	**killed in action**
1769	**Pte Garrett Hayden**	**killed in action**
1051	**Pte John Scanlon**	**killed in action**
1398	**Pte Joseph Williams**	**killed in action**
1328	**Lance-Sgt Thomas Williams**	**died of wounds**
1240	**Cpl William Allen**	**severely wounded**
1112	**Cpl John Lyons**	**dangerously wounded**
1362	**Pte Frederick Hitch**	**dangerously wounded**
716	**Pte Robert Jones**	**slightly wounded**
1812	**Pte William Tasker**	**slightly wounded**

Commissariat and Transport Department

Acting Storekeeper Louis Byrne	**killed in action**
Commissariat Officer James Dalton	**severely wounded**

Natal Mounted Police

Trooper Sydney Hunter	**killed in action**

Natal Native Contingent

Cpl Michael Anderson	**killed in action**
Pte Xhosa native	**killed in action**
Cpl Carl Scammel	**dangerously wounded**
Cpl Friedrich Schiess	**slightly wounded**

BIBLIOGRAPHY OF RESEARCH AND REFERENCE MATERIAL

ATTWOOD, Sgt F: Letter from Rorke's Drift dated 25th January 1879. Royal Corps of Transport Museum.

BOURNE, Lt-Col F: Article in 'The Listener' for 30th December 1936, taken from his radio broadcast ten days earlier.

CHARD, Lt J R M: Official report dated 25th January 1879. Published in newspapers in March 1879, and in The Royal Engineers' Journal for August 1879. An account submitted to Queen Victoria on 21st February 1880. The Silver Wreath.

CLARKE, Lt-Col W J; NMP: 'My Career in South Africa'. The Killie Campbell Library.

DUNNE, Lt-Col W A: 'Reminiscences of Campaigning in South Africa. 1877-81'. The Army Service Corps Journal (The Waggoner), for February 1892. Royal Corps of Transport Museum.

EMERY, F: 'The Red Soldier', London 1977.

FYNN, H F: 'My Recollections of a Famous Campaign'. The Natal Witness, 22nd January 1913.

HALL, R: Letter to The Natal Witness c 1906. Killie Campbell.

HALLAM-PARR, Cpt H: 'A Sketch of the Kaffir and Zulu Wars'.

HAMILTON-BROWNE, Col G: 'A Lost Legionary in South Africa'.

HARFORD, Col H: 'Zulu War Journal' of Col Henry Harford CB. Edited by Daphne Child. Pietermaritzburg, 1978.

HITCH, Pte F: Interview at Netley Hospital, published in 'The Cambrian' newspaper, Swansea, 13th June 1879.

An Original account held by the South Wales Borderers Museum.

HOLME, N: 'The Silver Wreath. Being the 24th Regiment at Isandhlwana and Rorke's Drift, 1879'. London 1979.

HOOK, Pte A H: 'How They Held Rorke's Drift'. Published in The Royal Magazine for February 1905.

His account in the Strand Magazine, 1891.

HOWARD, A: Letter in the Daily Telegraph, 25th March, 1879. J. M. – Natal Volunteer: 'Reminiscences of the Zulu War'. The Natal Witness – Killie Campbell Library.

JOBBINS, J: Letter from Rorke's Drift, published in the Hereford Times, 29th March 1879. The Red Soldier.

JONES, Pte R: His account in the Strand Magazine, 1891.

JONES, W: Account in his obituary in the Manchester Evening News, 16th April 1913.

His account in the Strand Magazine, 1891.

LABAND, J: 'Fight Us in the Open', Pietermaritzburg, 1985.

LONDON GAZETTE for 1879: Including VC citations dated 2nd May; 17th June; 17th November; and 29th November.

LUGG, H: Letter in the North Devon Herald Supplement, 24th April 1879.

LUGG, H C: 'A Natal Family Looks Back', Durban, 1970.

LUMMIS, Canon W: 'Padre George Smith of Rorke's Drift', Norwich, 1978.

LYONS, Cpl J: Interview at Netley, published in 'The Cambrian' newspaper, Swansea, 13th June 1879.

MASON, C: Letter from Rorke's Drift to his family in London. Dated 8th February 1879. National Army Museum.

MITFORD, B: 'Through the Zulu Country', London, 1883.

MORRIS, D: 'The Washing of the Spears', New York, 1965.

NORRIS-NEWMAN, C: 'In Zululand with the British throughout the Zulu War of 1879', London, 1880.
ORCHARD, G E: Letter from Rorke's Drift dated 29th January 1879, to his brother in Bedminster, Bristol, published in the Bristol Observer, 29th March, 1879.
PATON, G; GLENNIE, F; PENN-SYMONS, W: 'Historical Records of the 24th Regiment', London, 1892.
PENN-SYMONS, Capt W: Report written in 1879. The South Wales Borderers Museum, Brecon.
REYNOLDS, Surgeon-Major J H: Report to the Army Hospital's Dept. 1878-79. The Royal Army Medical Corps Journal.
SAVAGE, Pte E: Interview on his return to Brecon, 16th July 1879. Published in The Manchester Weekly Post, 19th July 1879.
SMITH, Rev G: Report dated 3rd February 1879. The Royal Army Chaplain's Department Journal for July 1936.
SMITH, Sgt G: Letter from Rorke's Drift dated 24th January 1879. Brecon County Times – The Red Soldier.
SMITH-DORRIEN, Gen H: 'Memories of Forty-Eight Years' Service', London, 1925.
SYMONS, J P: 'Reminiscences of the Zulu War', by a Natal Carbineer. Natal Witness – Killie Campbell Library.
WAR OFFICE PAPERS: Including 'The Narrative of the Field Operations connected with the Zulu War of 1879'. Published by the Intelligence Branch in 1881, and reprinted in 1907.
WATERS, Pte J: Interview at Netley Hospital, published in 'The Cambrian' newspaper, Swansea, 13th June 1879.
WILLIAMS, W A: 'The VC's of Wales and the Welsh Regiments', Wrexham, 1984.
WITT, Rev O: Statement given at Bramhall Hall in Cheshire in 1879.

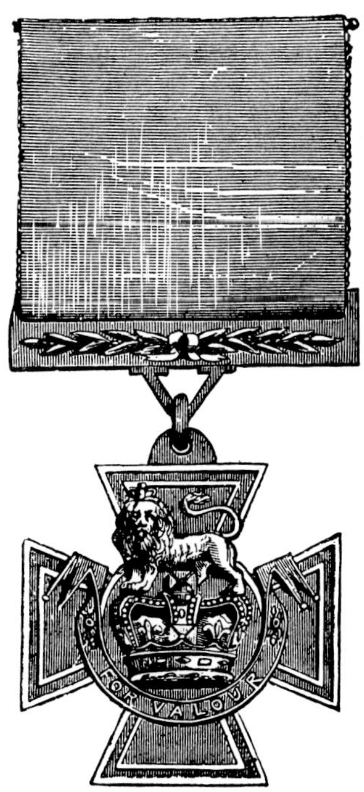

Index

AFRICAN BANTU

BRITAIN

BRITISH AND COLONIAL FORCES

FOREIGN LANDS

PERSONALITIES

RORKE'S DRIFT, ACTION AT:

RORKE'S DRIFT, DEFENDERS OF:

SOUTH AFRICA

ZULUS

MISCELLANEOUS

ACKNOWLEDGEMENTS

The Public Records Office, Kew.
The British Library Newspaper Library, Colindale.
The Killie Campbell Africana Library, Durban.
The Natal Archives Depot, Pietermaritzburg.
The Natal Midlands Branch of the Geneological Society of South Africa, Pietermaritzburg.
The National Army Museum, Chelsea.
The Imperial War Museum, London.
The South Wales Borderers Regimental Museum, Brecon.
The Royal Engineers Museum, Chatham.
The Royal Corps of Transport Regimental Museum, Aldershot.
The Royal Army Medical Corps Historical Museum, Aldershot.
The British Broadcasting Corporation.
The Staff of Manchester Central Library, Eccles Public Library, and various other libraries in Britain and South Africa.

Picture research was through Military Archive & Research Services, Braceborough, Lincolnshire. The publishers and researchers would like to thank the following individuals and organisations who kindly furnished illustrations for this book.

Reproduced by gracious permission of Her Majesty the Queen – Copyright reserved: p48, 84-85, 129b, 130, 136, 144, 149, 153, 154t.
J Bancroft: p39, 44, 53, 58 59, 61, 78t, 126, 132-133, 134, 139, 154b.
BBC Hulton Picture Library: p11, 13, 50-51, 80, 90-91, 98-99b, 102-103, 112-113, 156-157.
The Buffs and Canterbury Royal Museums: p21t.
H E R Bunting: p142, 143.
Gateshead Central Library: p122-123, 138.
Canon W Lummis: p125.
Killie Campbell Africana Library: p6-7, 12, 24-25b, 27, 31b, 36-37, 38, 52, 81, 92, 93, 97, 98-99t, 110, 146, 148.
Lancashire Library Services: p124.
J Maber Collection: p16.
Military Archive & Research Services: p8, 9, 22-23, 29, 32, 35, 66, 67, 72-73, 88tl, 103, 111, 114-115, 117, 119, 120-121, 131, 132, 137r.
National Army Museum: p2-3, 10, 17, 18-19, 21b, 24-25t, 26-27, 28, 30, 31t, 33, 34, 45, 46, 56, 82, 100-101, 104-105, 106-107, 108-109, 114, 116, 118, 127b, 135, 137.
The Royal Army Medical Corps Historical Museum: p87t, 129t.
The Sherwood Foresters Museum: p23, 94-95.
The South Wales Borderers & Monmouthshire Regimental Museum: p86, 87b, 88b, 140, 141, 145, 152, 155.
Spinks & Company: p88tr.
The Regimental Museum of the Royal Corps of Transport: p127t, 128.
C Wilkinson-Latham: p76, 78b.